NEW EVERYDAY ENGLISH

Book 4

NEW EVERYDAY ENGLISH

Book 4

English Textbook Committee

SHINGU PUBLISHING CO.

Introduction

The New Everyday English 4 textbook is designed for intermediate students who already have a basic knowledge of conversational English. It aims to meet the needs of college attendees from various backgrounds and fields of study. Students will develop communication skills by studying topic-oriented lessons. These lessons are structured upon topics and grammar principles. The text also attempts to meet student's interests and reduce their anxiety about studying another language.

New Everyday English 4 is organized into 12 units centered upon topics related to student life and real world situations. Each unit can be completed in a two-hour class or extended with supplementary material to suit longer periods.

This textbook also works in tandem with a companion online cyber learning program that provides students with self-study language lab material. Through the cyber learning program students can log on and prepare for the subject material of each unit before studying the book.

Furthermore, New Everyday English 4 contains a unified structure. Each unit is broken down in roughly the same way so that students and teachers alike will become familiar with the sequence of sections and know what to expect from unit to unit. Although the structure is the same throughout the book, the activities vary to help stimulate the students as they increase their speaking, listening, and reading skills. The structure of each unit is as follows.

Warm-up : Each unit begins with a warm up intended to draw the students' attention to the topic and subject matter in an interesting way.

This section is also intended to be flexible enough that teachers can adapt it to their own style or add and take what they see fit.

Vocabulary : Following the Warm up is a list of key topic-oriented words for the students to learn. Most of the vocabulary introduced will be used throughout the entire unit, so it is useful for the teacher to help students learn and apply these words as soon as possible.

Dialogue : In this section students study a real world dialogue by listening to the companion audio file. Following the listening segment they practice reading and speaking the script in pairs.

Grammar Focus : In this section key grammar points are explained with models, charts, and example sentences. The grammar is introduced with continuity and sequential learning in mind.

Reading/Listening : Each unit includes a reading (listening) comprehension text with a companion audio file. Students read (listen to) the text and then answer the following comprehension questions. The companion audio file can be used at any time throughout this exercise to help the students sound out and pronounce the text.

Speaking and Writing : In this section students ask and answer (write) topic oriented questions. It is intended to be flexible enough for students to practice short answer dialogues or extend the conversation into free talking sessions.

Editing : Each unit ends with exercises that enable the students to demonstrate their mastery of the language targets presented. The exercises range in style from editing, fill in the blank exercises, etc.

Review Units : Units 6 and 12 of New Everyday English 4 are review units. They depart from the structure just outlined and are comprised primarily of exercises based on what the students have learned up to that point. Review Units are intended to prepare students for exams as well as providing opportunity for teachers to check and gauge students' progress. Unit 6 reviews the content of Units 1 through 5 while Unit 12 reviews the content of units 7-11.

As every department and class has a different mix of students, teachers are encouraged to supplement the book with their own activities and ideas. The textbook committee also recommends feedback from both the teachers and the students.

Contents

Contents

Unit 01

Using a Dictionary

Warm-up : How well do you know the following words? If you know the word very well, write VW. If you know it, but not very well, write NVW. If you don't know the word at all, write NAA.

Unit 01

Cold ______ Have ______ Color ______ Record ______

Pretty ______ Skinny ______ Dish ______ Funny ______

Now answer the questions about the words

1. How many different meanings does cold have as an adjective? Is cold also a noun or an adverb?

2. How many meanings do you think the word "have" has? Write down 5 different meanings for "have" with examples. Eg. to eat-I had eggs for breakfast. to drink-I had a cup of coffee.

Using a Dictionary

3. Is there another way to spell color? Make a sentence with color as a verb.

4. How are the verb and noun pronunciations of "record" different?

5. What does "pretty" mean in the following sentences:

a) I'm pretty certain I will go to Europe this summer.

b) He is pretty ugly.

6. Is pretty used more in written or spoken English?

7. Is the meaning of "skinny" good, bad, or neutral?

8. What does dish mean in the following sentences:

a) I ate a vegetarian dish.

b) She's a real dish!

9. Does "funny" mean the same as interesting?

10. Does "funny" usually mean "strange" in written or spoken English?

Vocabulary : Dictionaries are full of abbreviations. With a partner, guess the meaning of the following abbreviations.

1. BrE — British English
2. PHR V —
3. IrishE —
4. IDM —
5. AmE —
6. Sth —
7. Pl. —
8. ScotE —
9. Sb —
10. NZE —
11. Sing. —
12. AustralE —

Unit 01

Dialogue 1 : Complete the dialogue using the following vocabulary

useful	realized	bookshelf	hurry	alphabetically

Sumin: Wow. Is that an old dictionary?

Jungmin: No, it's a book dictionary, but it's not old. It's an advanced learner's dictionary. Have you ever used one?

Sumin: No, my father has a couple of Korean-English and English-Korean dictionaries on his *(1)*_________, but they haven't been used in years. How do you use it?

Jungmin: When you want to find out the meaning of a word, you have to look it up *(2)*_________. For example, for the word "dictionary" first you look under "d", then "i", then "c" and so on.

Sumin: Why don't you just use your smart phone's dictionary? Doesn't it take a lot longer using the book?

Jungmin: I use my smart phone when I'm in a *(3)*________ or when I don't have this dictionary around, but I find the book dictionary a little more *(4)*________ than most electronic dictionaries.

Sumin: How is that possible?

Jungmin: Well, it is a lot more in-depth. There are more meanings for the words and more examples of usage. Plus, because it's also a learner's dictionary, there is a section on phrasal verbs, collocations, linking words, and idioms.

Sumin: I never *(5)*________ what a good learning tool a dictionary could be.

Dialogue 1- Questions

1. Does Sumin use a book dictionary?

2. When does Jungmin use his smart phone dictionary?

3. Why does Jungmin prefer his learner's dictionary to his smart phone dictionary?

Dialogue 2

Heejung: What's wrong?

Jinwoo: My teacher told me "cunning" isn't good English. He said it's Konglish, but I found it in the dictionary.

Heejung: Yes, but Koreans usually use cunning to mean "cheating." Have you looked up the meaning in the dictionary yet?

Jinwoo: I am doing it right now.

Heejung: How many different meanings are there?

Jinwoo: Two: both say an ability to get what you want, especially by tricking or lying, but one is a noun and the other is an adjective.

Heejung: Let me see. Look. See the examples? Koreans usually use it alone. "Don't be cunning." In the examples it says 'Cunning as a fox, a cunning liar, it took energy and cunning to win.'

Jinwoo: Yeah, it's a bit different than the way Koreans use it.

Heejung: I always look at the examples in the dictionary. They help me learn how to use the words.

Unit 01

Dialogue 2- Questions

1. What is the Konglish meaning of "cunning?"

2. What is the English meaning of "cunning?"

3. What does Heejung look at to help her learn how to use new words?

Unit 01

Using a Dictionary

Grammar : More Phrasal Verbs

A dictionary will show you if a phrasal verb is separable or inseparable.

- *Turn sth on* — Turn the computer on **or** Turn on the computer.
- *Look for sb/sth* — I looked for my dog everywhere. Can you look for my keys?

Use your dictionary and put the word "it" in the correct place.

1. You look so hot with that parka on. Why don't you take ________ off?
2. Your jacket is so dirty. Just look at ________!
3. I haven't finished my sandwich yet. Don't throw ________ away.
4. The TV is too loud. Please turn ________ down.
5. Jeju will be a really fun trip. I'm really looking forward to ________.
6. Is that story about you forgetting your homework true, or did you make ________ up?
7. I saw a really cool hat at the store. I tried ________ on but it was too big.
8. Don't throw your tissue on the floor. Pick ________ up!
9. I need my electronic dictionary for my homework. Please give ________ back.
10. If you don't know the answer to the homework, you have to figure ________ out yourself. I can't help you!

Reading : Pre-reading questions

1. The first complete dictionary was the Oxford English Dictionary. How many years did it take to write?
2. How did people find word meanings before dictionaries were invented?
3. What are 4 things you can use dictionaries for?

Read the story about dictionaries and answer the questions.

Before dictionaries were invented, how did people know how to spell words? If they were reading a book and saw a word they didn't know, how did they find out its meaning? If they wanted to know how to pronounce a word, how could they find out? What about if they wanted to know what kind of word it was, or how to use it properly in a sentence?

The only way people could find answers to these questions was to talk to other writers or to find the word being used in other books, letters, or writing. This could take a lot of time.

The first English dictionaries were made by individuals and were not perfect because they were missing so many words, contained many misspellings, and were considered by English scholars to be incomplete.

In 1857, a group of British writers were fed up with the dictionaries available, and they decided to organize a society to make a comprehensive dictionary. Research began in 1860 and hundreds of scholars began working on gathering all the words in the English language. The final chapters of the dictionary were completed in 1928. The dictionary was named the Oxford English Dictionary (OED).
After 20 years, the dictionary needed to be updated, so a second edition was started. This included new forms of English from countries like India,

Australia, New Zealand, South Africa, and the Caribbean. In the end, it was finally completed in 1986 and contained 17 volumes.

Currently, the entire OED has been computerized and updated. It contains over 600,000 words.

Reading - Questions

1. What was wrong with the first dictionaries?

2. How many people worked on the OED?

3. How long did it take before the OED needed to be updated?

4. What countries' forms of English were included in the 2nd edition?

Speaking : What part of speech are the following words?

Bread- noun	Sexy-	On -	Fast
Shrunk -	Slowly-	Sometimes -	Funny

The following words have more than one meaning. Write two different sentences using two different meanings.

1. Book Meaning 1: Meaning 2:
2. Kind Meaning 1: Meaning 2:
3. Can Meaning 1: Meaning 2:
4. Play Meaning 1: Meaning 2:
5. Mean Meaning 1: Meaning 2:
6. Ring Meaning 1: Meaning 2:
7. Bum Meaning 1: Meaning 2:
8. Gay Meaning 1: Meaning 2:

Editing : Correct the following sentences.

1. Why are you watching TV when you have homework to do? Please turn off it!

2. I'm hungry. Let's go to eat out!

3. Why are you wearing your jacket inside? Please take off it.

4. The fighting couple should make with each other up.

5. My friend lives 1 floor above me. Let's go to his place up and see what he's doing.

Unit 01

Unit 02

Slang and Idioms

Warm-up : What is an idiom(숙어)? It is a group of words that makes an expression. The expression's meaning is very different than the meanings of the individual words.

> **Eg.** "The cat is out of the bag" means everyone knows the secret. And "She wears the pants" in their relationship, means she controls her boyfriend or husband.

What is slang(속어/슬랭)? It is a nonstandard variety of speech used by subcultures. It consists of words and phrases that change very frequently.

> **Eg.** in the 1930s, men called pretty girls "dolls" in the 1950s and 60s, "chicks" in the 1980s and 90s, "babes", and nowadays you hear, "hotties" and "Phat".

What is an adage(속담)? It is an old expression that expresses a truth. A proverb is the same.

Examples of adages are "Fixing the barn door after the cow has escaped." Or, "You can lead a horse to water, but you can't make it drink.

Look at the underlined words in the following sentences and write Idiom (I), Slang (S) or Adage (A) beside them.

1. If I go to Garden 5, I can go shopping and see a movie. I can kill two birds with one stone! ________
2. You don't want to go to the beach. You are so lame! It's a beautiful day. Let' s go. ________
3. His mom died and he also just lost his job. When it rains, it pours! ________
4. Hey, I know you're angry, but take it easy. Everything will be OK. ________
5. Dude! Let's go the bar and get Crunk. ________
6. Park Jisung is a sick soccer player. ________
7. He's pretty angry this morning. He must have slept on the wrong side of the bed. ________
8. An alien ate your homework? Give me a break! ________
9. He is so two-faced! He'll say one thing to you and another to his friends. ________
10. You think his life is so good because the grass is always greener on the other side of the fence. ________

Unit 02

Unit 02

Slang and Idioms

Vocabulary : First, translate the following words into Korean. Then, use them to fill in the blanks.

regional	phrasal verb	misuse	out-of-date	clear and concise
simile	fluent	impress	realistic	expression

1. A verb which has a preposition or an adverb attached like "look up" or "take back" is a ________________
2. When you compare two things using the words "like", "as", or "than" it is called a ________________ .
3. He tries to ________________ girls with his expensive car and clothes.
4. You are 156cm but you want to be a flight attendant? You must be more ________________ .
5. Jeju Air is a ________________ airline. They only fly in Korea and a few other countries like China, Japan, and South-east Asia.
6. This textbook was printed in 1988. It's really ________________ .
7. She is always so ________________ when she does her presentation in class so everyone always understands her.
8. She lived in Japan for a long time so her Japanese is almost perfectly ________________ .
9. Don't ________________ the money I gave you for your new textbooks. Don't use it to drink soju with your friends!
10. Her English is good but sometimes she uses funny ________________s that I've never heard before.

Dialogue 1 : Read the following dialogues and answer the questions about them.

Wangju: Wow! It's really raining cats and dogs today, isn't it?

John: What?

Wangju: I said it's really raining cats and dogs··· Why are you smiling? Isn't that the correct expression?

John: The expression is right, but it's old and out-of-date. Not even my grandmother uses it anymore.

Wangju: But I learned it in this new book about English idioms. Here, take a look at it.

(Gives book to John who begins to look at it)

John: Another problem with learning idioms and slang is they go out-of-date really fast. Look at this one "Crikey do I ever feel crook today!" That's Australian English. A lot of Americans wouldn't understand it. That's because a lot of slang and idioms are regional.

Dialogue 1- Questions

1. Why is John smiling at Wangju?

2. What are two problems of learning slang and idioms?

Dialogue 2

Wangju: So you think I'm wasting my time?

John: Idioms can be fun to learn, but in my opinion, learning to speak clear and concise English is better.

Wangju: But my friends all say idioms are important if I want to speak like a native speaker.

John: But you aren't a native speaker.

Wangju: But it is my goal to speak like one.

John: Do you think your goal is realistic?

Wangju: It is difficult.

John: What is your purpose for learning English? Is it to impress people by speaking perfectly fluent English, or to speak clearly and concisely so other English speakers can understand you?

Wangju: So I shouldn't learn idioms?

John: No, but you shouldn't spend too much time on them. Try studying stuff like phrasal verbs. They are hard to learn, but much more useful.

Wangju: Thanks for your advice!

Dialogue 2 - Questions

1. What is Wangju's goal for studying English?

2. Does John think Wangju's goal is realistic?

3. Does John think learning idioms is a waste of time?

4. What does he think Wangju should study instead?

Grammar: Phrasal Verbs

A phrasal verb is two words—usually a verb and a preposition—that act like one word. The meaning of the verb changes when you add the preposition.

Eg. look–I am looking at my brother.

look after–I am looking after my brother.

"Look" and "Make" are two verbs that have many phrasal combinations. Match the phrasal verbs with their meanings and then complete the sentences using them.

1. look up ____	**a.** to look at something in the future with positive expectation
2. make up ____	**b.** to search for an object
3. look out ____	**c.** to change something into something else
4. look forward to ____	**d.** to search for a word, phone number, or address
5. look for ____	**e.** to investigate something
6. make for ____	**f.** to warn someone about something
7. look into ____	**g.** to say sorry to someone after a fight
8. make into ____	**h.** to move towards a location

Unit 02

1. We ________________ the summer vacation

2. The police must ________________ last night's murder.

3. She is trying to ________________ her husband ________________ a gentleman.

4. I want to ________________ my high school friend when I go home next weekend.

5. After you get to the top of the mountain, ________________ the river and I'll meet you at the boat.

6. The fighting couple needs to ________________ before their children get home from school.

7. Help me ________________ my homework. I can't find it and I'm going to school soon.

8. ________________! The crazy teacher is coming.

Listening : Listen to the two friends talking about studying idioms and answer the following questions.

1. What does tossing and turning mean?
2. What does Chris think is easy to misuse?
3. Who told Jieun learning idioms is important?
4. Does Chris think learning idioms is realistic?
5. What kind of English does Chris think Jieun should learn?

Turn to the transcript section at back of the book and practice reading the dialogue with your partner.

Speaking : Similes are used very often in English. Animal similes are fixed–so if a friend is very quiet, we would say, *he's as quiet as a mouse*, not, he's as quiet as a cat. Here are a list of adjectives and animals. Match them together.

1. As blind as a ______________ ox
2. As hungry as a ______________ owl
3. As busy as a ______________ bat
4. As tall as a ______________ snail
5. As wise as an ______________ bee
6. As strong as an ______________ giraffe
7. As sly as a ______________ horse
8. As proud as a ______________ peacock
9. As slow as a ______________ koala
10. As sleepy as a ______________ fox

Now practice the similes. One student closes their book. The other reads the following sentences.

Unit 02

Student with book	Student without book
"He is very quiet."	"Yes, he's as quiet as a mouse."

1. He is always hungry.
2. My mother is very busy.
3. Your boyfriend is so tall.
4. The student is very sly.
5. My father is very proud.
6. My grandmother is very wise.
7. His glasses are so thick.
8. She is always sleeping in my class.
9. Hurry up. Don't be so slow.
10. He's always lifting weights in the gym.

Unit 02

Slang and Idioms

Editing : Fix the following sentences.

1. You can look in his address on the internet.

2. She looked up her bag under her bed.

3. The bus driver drives slow as a snail as.

4. Many classic movies aren't in color, they are in white and black.

5. My father is as busy as a fox.

Unit 03

Dialects

Warm-up : There are many different kinds of English in the world: Australian, American, British, Jamaican, and Indian are a few of the nationalities that speak different kinds of English. Even in one country people speak many varieties of English. For example, in America, people in New York City, Boston, Texas, and California all speak different dialects.

Unit 03

Read the following English expressions from the different countries and guess the meaning of the underlined words and expressions.

1. Australia: He's my best <u>mate</u> ________
2. England: I'm going out to buy a pack of <u>fags</u>. ________
3. Singapore: He always likes <u>to action</u> in front of girls! ________
4. Scotland: Alright children, do you <u>kin</u> what a said? ________
5. Britain or Australia: I'm moving to London next week and need to <u>let a flat</u>. ________
6. Canada: It's a real nice car, <u>eh</u>? ________
7. Australia: <u>G'day</u>! How was your weekend? ________

8. England: Have you sussed out the crossword puzzle yet? ________

9. Britain and Australia: I like to eat crisps when I drink beer. ________

10. Scotland: A'm tint! Can you tell me where the movie theater is? ________

a) cigarettes	b) I'm lost	c) isn't it?	d) figured out
e) hello	f) potato chips	g) show off	h) friend
i) understand	j) rent an apartment		

Guess the meanings of the following five British, Australian and New Zealand expressions!

1. Well, I have to go now. Cheerio!
2. Teacher, may I go to the loo, please?
3. When I was swimming, someone nicked my wallet!
4. Let's go to the pub. I just got paid so I'll shout you the first drink.
5. I worked for 12 hours today. I'm completely knackered!

Vocabulary : Look up the following words in a English-Korean dictionary. Then, complete the sentences using the correct words.

pronounce	standard	accent	regional
Queen's English	expression	varieties	common

1. The Busan dialect has a very strong ______________ .

2. In England, there are many ______________ of English.

3. "Cheers!" is a British ______________ which means "thank you!"

4. In America, the ______________ dialect, also called General American English, is the Midwestern dialect.

5. In Korean, 안녕하세요! is a very ______________ expression that you hear everyday.

6. Korean dialects are ______________: Gyungsan, Chungcheung, Jeolla, Jeju, Seoul, Gangwan, and North Korean.

7. When Japanese learn English, they cannot ______________ "th" and "r" very well.

8. Many rich people in England speak the ______________ dialect.

Dialogue 1 : Fill in the blanks with the correct questions.

For example / Is Australian English different from American English?/ What are you studying? But why are you studying Australian English?

Unit 03

Suji: Wow! You're studying hard as usual.

*(1)*______________________?

Sungmin: It's a book about Australian English expressions.

Suji: *(2)*____?

Sungmin: Yes, it's a completely different dialect. The pronunciation and expressions are both very different.

Suji: *(3)*____?

Sungmin: Well, in American English, people say friend, but in Australia, they say mate. In America, they say, "I'm sick." But in Australia they say, "I'm crook."

Suji: You really learn fast!

*(4)*______________________________?

Sungmin: Two reasons: first, I'm going for a 4 week trip to Australia next month. Second, I hope to work at a resort in Bali next year and most of the foreign tourists who go there are Australians.

Dialogue 1- Questions

1. What kind of book is Sungmin studying?

2. Is American English similar to Australian English?

3. Will studying Australian English be useful for Sungmin? Why or why not?

Dialogue 2 : Fill in the blanks with the missing words and practice the dialogue with your partner twice.

Hiyeon: What's wrong Sunghee?

Sunghee: I'm reading about English *(1)* d_______________s. There are so many of them. Sometimes, I think I speak English pretty *(2)*_______________, but when I read about all the different dialects and *(3)* a_______________s, I think it's hopeless.

Hiyeon: Don't think that way. Try to be more positive. You've come so far from one year ago. Plus dialects aren't really that important.

Sunghee: Why *(4)*_______________?

Hiyeon: Do you plan on living overseas?

Sunghee: No.

Hiyeon: Why are you learning English *(5)*______________?

Sunghee: I really want to work in the hotel industry, plus I want to travel.

Hiyeon: In a hotel, what nationalities will be *(6)* sp______________ing English with you mostly?

Sunghee: Probably Chinese, Japanese, and Americans.

Hiyeon: See··· most people who travel to Korea aren't even *(7)* n______________e English speakers. They speak English as a second language like you do. And most native speakers who travel don't speak with *(8)* h______________y accents. They speak international English. So don't worry too much. Dialects are fun to learn, but unless you are going to live overseas or work with many people who speak a dialect, it's not so *(9)* i______________t to learn.

Sunghee: Right. Just learning to speak a *(10)* s______________d English should be good enough for working at a hotel or travelling!

Unit 03

Dialogue 2- Questions

1. Why is Sunghee unhappy?

2. Why is Sunghee learning English?

3. When does Hiyeon think it is a good idea to study an English dialect?

Unit 03 Dialects

Grammar : Adverbs have many different kinds of meanings. The most common are…

1. **Manner:** well, slowly, easily, carefully, etc.
2. **Place:** here, there, above, below, between
3. **Time:** now, then, later, soon
4. **Degree:** very, really, too, so
5. **Frequency:** never, always, sometimes, rarely, usually

** There are other types of adverbs, length of time, linking, comment or attitude, viewpoint, and many others.

Read the following sentences and underline the adverbs. Then write down what kind of adverb it is (some sentences have more than one).

Eg. She is <u>very</u> pretty. – degree

1. How long have you lived there? –
2. I did my homework yesterday. –
3. She sometimes drinks soju with her classmates. –
4. You need to go upstairs. –
5. The teacher spoke too quickly –
6. My boyfriend often dances with me slowly. –
7. He arrived very late. –
8. The dog ran fast. –
9. The student was quite pleased with her test score. –
10. You must go home right now. –

Some adverbs and adjectives have the same form. For example, fast.

Adjective — He is fast. Adverb — He ran fast.

If the word is an adjective, it will appear with the "be" verb. If the word is an adverb, it will usually modify an action verb.

Make sentences with the following words as ADVERBS!

1. — near
2. — late
3. — pretty
4. — early
5. — straight

Reading : **Before starting the reading, in groups of 3 or 4, try to answer the following questions as best as you can.**

1. How many different dialects are there in Korea?
2. Can you, your parents, or grandparents speak any non-standard Korean dialects?
3. What is the standard dialect of Korea?
4. What dialect sounds the coolest to you? What one sounds the strangest to you?
5. What do you think is going to happen to Korean dialects in the future?

Unit 03

Dialects

The Korean language has many different dialects. Most of the dialects are regional. These include Hamgyong, Hwanghae, Gangwon, Chungcheong, Gyungsan, Jeolla, and Jeju dialects, but the standard dialect used by all news anchors and TV shows is the Seoul dialect.

The influence of TV is one reason many people believe Korean dialects are dying and will disappear in the future. Another reason is the large number of people who have moved from the countryside to live in the Seoul area since the 1970s. 44 year old Kim Young-nam remembers growing up in Seoul after moving from Mokpo when he was a middle school student. "I had a heavy Jeolla accent when I first moved to Seoul in 1983 but the other students would tease me and call me 'country boy' , so I stopped using it and tried to sound like the rest of the students."

His father also had a difficult time at work. "Even though he was very smart and was hired as a salaryman at LG, his boss didn't like it when he spoke with his Jeolla dialect. He worked hard for 7 years and didn't get promoted once. So when he quit and changed jobs, he tried really hard to speak in the Seoul dialect."

Young children in Jeju today watch a lot of Korean dramas where everyone speaks with a Seoul dialect. "Seoul people sound so cool. Whenever there is a character speaking with a Jeju dialect, usually they are a farmer or someone stupid." Says middle school student, Jo Eun-bi. "I want to sound like the announcers or like a city girl, not a stupid country girl!"

Will dialects die? "I hope not" says Korean language major, Lee Ha-na. "If people only speak with a Seoul dialect, it would be a lot more boring, like going to a restaurant and only having one dish on the menu. A variety of dialects and accents makes life more interesting."

1. What are some reasons people stop using their home dialects? Do you think this is still true today?
2. Do the Korean schools need to protect dialects? Should the government help?
3. Would Korea be better or worse if there was only one dialect? What would be good and what would be bad?

Speaking

Student A : Look up the following British words with your smart phone:

cheeky windscreen git knickers lorry

Student B : Look up the following Australian words with your smart phone:

fairdinkum yobbo heaps Pommy sunnies

Unit 03

Write some sentences using the words and read them to your partner. The student who guesses the most meanings correctly wins.

Editing : Correct the following sentences.

1. She is woke up late today.
2. My grandmother is very kindly.
3. He ran fastly all the way to school.
4. I hardly never smoke cigarettes.
5. The students changed clothes very fastly.

Unit 04

Pronunciation

Warm-up : With a partner, complete the following questions about learning pronunciation. After you finish, the teacher will discuss the answers with the class.

1. It is impossible to learn perfect pronunciation unless you start learning English when you are a child.

a) Agree b) Disagree c) Not sure

2. Perfect pronunciation is more important than being understood when speaking a language.

a) Agree b) Disagree c) Not sure

3. Pronunciation teaching should start with listening, not speaking.

a) Agree b) Disagree c) Not sure

4. American Standard English is the best model for teaching pronunciation.

a) Agree b) Disagree c) Not sure

5. Learning word stress and intonation are more important than leaning phonetics.

a) Agree b) Disagree c) Not sure

6. Students should all learn phonetic symbols ( )

a) Agree b) Disagree c) Not sure

7. Learning spelling is part of learning pronunciation.

a) Agree b) Disagree c) Not sure

8. Native speakers of English are usually white.

a) Agree b) Disagree c) Not sure

Vocabulary

Match the term with it's Korean translation.

1. Phonetics — 자음

2. Stress — 유창한

3. Vowels — 음성학

4. Consonants — 음절

5. Intonation — 발음

6. Pronunciation — 억양

7. Syllable — 모음

8. Fluent — 강세

Complete the sentences using the vocabulary.

1. Her son is only 8 years old but he is ________________ in Korean, English, and Japanese.

2. A, E, I, O, U, and sometimes Y are ________________ and the rest of the letters of the alphabet are ________________ .
3. The word "beautiful" is made up of 3 ______________________ .
4. She doesn't understand English very well but she speaks with good ______________________ .
5. To learn pronunciation, children must start with ________________ and learn each sound.
6. In English, both words and sentences have ________________ .
7. ________________ is how the tone goes up or down when you are speaking.

Dialogue 1 : **Read the dialogue with a partner twice and answer the questions afterwards.**

Junyoung: You look like your working hard. What are you doing?

Heeyeon: I'm studying pronunciation.

Junyoung: What is that? That doesn't look like English.

Heeyeon: It's the phonetic alphabet. I'm studying it to help learn how to say new words I look up in a dictionary.

Junyoung: You think learning pronunciation will help you speak fluently like a native speaker?

Heeyeon: No, of course not. But it will help my listening and it will also help improve my speaking.

Junyoung: I really want to speak perfectly like a native speaker!

Heeyeon: That's silly. You don't need to speak perfect English to be understood and respected. Many famous non-native speakers didn't speak English perfectly but are famous for speaking well.

Junyoung: Really? Like who?

Heeyeon: Henry Kissinger was a U.S. Secretary of State and Gimun Ban is the head of the UN. They both speak English with heavy accents but are very good communicators.

Dialogue 1- Questions

1. Why is Heeyeon learning the phonetic alphabet?

2. Why does Junyoung want to learn pronunciation?

3. Who are some famous non-native speakers of English who didn' t speak English fluently but were very good at communicating?

Unit 04

Translate the following phonetic words into English.

1. læŋgwɪdʒ –	**2.** dɪkʃənərɪ –	**3.** əʊvəsiːz –	**4.** yunə'vɜrsɪti –
5. 'sɒkər –	**6.** θiətər –	**7.** 'ti,ʃɜrt –	**8.** 'ɒktəpəs –

Dialogue 2

Juno: Do you know about word stress?

Minhee: I hardly know anything.

Juno: Well, if you want to learn English vocabulary well, you' ll need to learn about wordstress.

Minhee: What do you mean?

Juno: Listen carefully—Japan and Japanese.

Minhee: What?

Juno: I'll say them again slowly. Japan has two syllables—Ja··· pan. The first syllable isn't stressed but the second is. But Japanese has three syllables—Ja··· pa···nese. The first syllable is stressed, but the second and third aren't.

Minhee: Why is that important?

Juno: Well, if you say a word and stress the wrong syllable, someone might not understand what you're saying.

Minhee: How do you learn where the word stress is?

Juno: When you study vocabulary, you can find out where the stress is by looking in your dictionary.

Dialogue 2 - Questions

1. Why is leaning word stress important?

2. Where can you find out about word stress?

Look up the following words in a dictionary and put the stress over the correct syllable.

1. photography	**2.** photograph	**3.** dialects	**4.** evil
5. Korean	**6.** recording	**7.** blackboard	**8.** diamond

Grammar: More Adverbs!

There are many different kinds of adverbs: manner, time, place, degree, frequency, linking, comment or attitude, adding or limiting, length of time, and viewpoint. There are three main positions in a sentence for adverbs:

1. **Front position:** Sometimes, I go to bed early.
2. **Middle position:** I sometimes go to bed early.
3. **End position:** I go to bed early, sometimes.

Some adverbs can go in different positions. Some can only go in one position.

Put the adverb in the correct place in the sentence. Sometimes more than one place is possible.

1. The book was interesting. (really)

2. Mr. Gibson, can you help me? My name is Mr. Olson, not Mr. Gibson. (actually)

3. I gave my phone number to one boy. (only)

4. I didn't like the concert. I didn't like it. (either)

5. Byungchan really likes Haesu. Really? Youngju really likes her. (too)

6. When we walked outside it began to rain. (suddenly)

7. When my grandfather felt pain in his chest I called an ambulance. (immediately)

Unit 04

8. My best friend and I went to school. (together)

9. I lost my wallet last night. Somebody found it and gave it to the police. (fortunately)

10. My friends all love singing, Minsu. (especially)

Listening : Intonation is a change in the pitch. It affects the meaning of a sentence. Listen to your teacher say the following sentences. How is the meaning different?

1a. I like Rain's music and movies.
1b. I like Rain's music··· and movies
2a. I'm not dating him because of his looks.
2b. I'm not dating him··· because of his looks!
3a. Let's eat, mom.
3b. Let's eat mom.
4a. A woman without her man··· is nothing!
4b. A woman: without her··· man is nothing!
5a. MaryJane and I went to school together.
5b. Mary, Jane, and I went to school together.

Speaking : In English certain words are stressed in a sentence. The meaning of a question can change depending on which words are stressed.

Eg. Did your mother go to Jeju **last** summer?

No, she went to Jeju **this** summer.

Or Did you mother go to **Jeju** last summer?

No, she went to **Gyungju**.

With a partner, take turns asking questions with the correct stress and using negative answers. Respond correctly.

1. Did you study in the library **this morning**?

   No…

2. You have **2** brothers, right?

   No…

3. Is that Professor Kim's **wife**?

   No…

4. Do you want to buy the red **shoes**?

   No…

5. You said your **boyfriend** is a doctor?

   No…

6. Would you like me to call John **and** Peter?

   No…

7. Are you learning **English** at an academy?

   No…

8. You said you are going to America to **learn English**?

   No…

9. Is Chris the teacher who is always reading **comic books**?

   No…

Unit 04

10. Is that <u>Sunna</u> wearing the white dress and eating pizza at the table?
No···

A person's tone can change the meaning of a sentence. For example, if you meet an old friend unexpectedly who you haven't seen in a long time, you'll say "Hi!" a lot different than you do to a classmate you see every day or an old girlfriend who dumped you.

Mark the intonation with arrows going up, down or straight and then practice the following conversations with your partner with the correct intonation.

Conversation 1

A: (politely) Beer?
B: (firmly) No thanks. I don't like beer.
A: (surprised) Are you sure?
B: (thinking about it) Well···
A: Here you are.
B: Thanks. (Drinks it in one shot).
A: (sarcastically) You don't like beer!

Conversation 2

A: (expecting agreement) You think Kim Yeon-ah is pretty, don't you?
B: (firmly) No, not really.

A: (shocked) What? Are you serious?

B: (sarcastically) Yeah, she's really really ugly.

A: (surprised) What?

B: (laughing) Just joking!

Editing : Fix the following sentences.

1. I enjoyed the TV show really.
2. Never I will smoke cigarettes.
3. I usually sometimes go to the nightclub.
4. He drinks on only Saturday night.
5. She leaves her sometimes home before 7a.m.

Unit 04

Unit 05

Konglish

Warm-up : What is Konglish? Sometimes Konglish words are English words and expressions borrowed by Koreans but used differently in Korea and sometimes they are new compound words made up by Koreans.

Look carefully at the following sentences? If there is a grammar mistake, underline the mistake and put a “GM” beside it. If there is a Konglish word used, underline it and put a “K” beside it. If there is both a grammar mistake and a Konglish word used, put a “B” beside it. If there are no Konglish or grammar mistakes, put an “A” beside it.

1. He drank too much soju so he is very drunken. _____
2. They went to a booking nightclub and met a couple of very good-looking guys. _____
3. He is more better looking than the talent. _____
4. I met the famous Korean singer on the street and got his sign. _____
5. After I brush my teeth, I like to gargle with mouthwash. _____
6. I am going to buy an apartment next year. _____

7. The panties he bought were too small, so he returned them to the store. _____

8. On Saturday, I stayed home and played the computer all day. _____

9. I was stressful in the meeting. _____

10. The mother played with her children after dinner. _____

First, check your answers with your classmates and then with your teacher. After checking, try correcting the answers with grammar mistakes and try changing the Konglish to Standard English.

Vocabulary : Use a dictionary and translate the following words and phrases into Korean. Then complete the problems.

misuse	coined	awkward
abbreviation	contraction	meaning
borrowed words	collocation	

Unit 05

1. Science Fiction writers have ________________ed many words like cyberspace, robotics, genetic engineering, and computer virus.

2. "I played with my university friends last Friday night" is not ungrammatical but it sounds very ____________ .

3. English has ________________ ________________ from other languages like French, Japanese, and Spanish.

4. All languages have ________________s. In English, "isn't", "aren't", "there's", and "won't" are some examples.

5. Sometimes the ________________ of a word changes. For example, "girl" used to mean a young person, male or female. Now it only means a young female.

6. It is easy to ________________ like "borrow" and "lend." Many

ESL students say, "I borrowed my friend 10 dollars" when they should say "I lent my friend 10 dollars."

7. Konglish is full of ________________ like "remote con" and "cream sand" as well as ________________ like "MT" and "SF".

8. When two words belong together it is called a ________________.

Dialogue 1 : **Read the following dialogues and fill in the blanks with the following words. Then practice them with your partner and answer the questions about the dialogues.**

coins, funny, ex-pats, be careful, studying, changed, native, consistently

Eunbi: Wow. I thought you were a *(1)*________________ English speaker.

John: I am.

Eunbi: But you just used a Konglish word.

John: So? Here in Korea, everyone including *(2)*________________ understand it, so I use it.

Eunbi: But isn't "eye-shopping" bad English?

John: Well, it's not how we use it but as long as Koreans use it *(3)*________________ and understand each other, it seems OK to me.

Eunbi: What about if I'm travelling or living abroad?

John: In that case, you have to *(4)*_______________. Unless you are speaking with Koreans or foreigners who've lived in Korea before, most people might not understand or they'll find it strange or funny.

Dialogue 1 - Questions

1. How does Eunbi feel when she hears John using Konglish?

2. What does John think about using Konglish?

3. When does John say Eunbi must be careful about using Konglish?

Dialogue 2

Unit 05

So-young: Hey! Why are you *(1)*_______________ Konglish?

John: I find it really interesting and fun.

So-young: Really? Why is that?

John: First of all, it *(2)*_______________ many new words like "open car" and "y-shirt" which sound kind of cool even though using them is awkward at first.

So-young: How do you say those words in Standard English?

John: We say, "convertible" and "dress-shirt."

So-young: "Dress-shirt" sounds *(3)*_______________. It's a dress and a shirt!

John: Haha! I never thought of it that way. Another thing that is interesting about it is it abbreviates many words we don't abbreviate in English, like "ball-pen", "clip", and "coating". We say, "ball-point pen", "paperclip", and "plastic coating."

So-young: I always thought Konglish was bad English but you've *(4)*_______________ my mind!

Dialogue 2 - Questions

1. Why is John studying Konglish?

2. What does Konglish do that makes it interesting?

3. How did So-young feel about Konglish before she talked to John?

4. How does she feel now?

Grammar : A collocation is two or more words that go together. For example, the word "have" goes together with both drinks and food.

Eg. Have a cup of coffee. Have a coke. Have dinner. Have a hamburger. But eat only goes with solid foods and not drinks.
Correct collocation: He ate some bibimbap.
Incorrect collocation: He ate a cup of coffee.

How can students learn collocations? Some collocations are very easy and obvious. "marry" is only used for humans. You can't marry a tree. "Climb" is usually used with objects with height like trees, mountains, or walls. However, some collocations are tricky. You can "make" a doghouse or a cake, but you can't "make" a building. You "build" a building.

First, when you learn a new word, write down other words that collocate with it. Rain heavily, strongly, lightly(but not strangely!). Second, read a lot. Students who read will see collocations used naturally and correctly. Third, learn collocations in groups like weather, family, personality, etc. Finally, use a good collocation website or dictionary.

Family Word Collocation Practice

Circle the correct word

1. The ring was her grandmother's, then her mother's, and now it is hers. It's a family jewel/heirloom/legend.
2. The extended/nuclear/wonderful family includes only the parents and their children. Not the uncles, aunts, cousins, or grandparents.
3. He has no brothers or sisters. He is an only/adult/immediate child.
4. He is my mother's uncle's nephew's wife. She is my far/blood/distant relative.
5. I am 20 and my brother is 24. He is my senior/elder/boss brother.
6. My mother quit her job and stayed at home to grow/feed/raise the children.
7. My uncles, aunts, cousins and grandparents all meet once every 5 years for a family wedding/picnic/reunion at my grandfather's farm.
8. My mother and father got divorced and me and my brother live with her. She is a solo/single/lonely parent.
9. When the children are bad, the parents must punish/kill/reward them.
10. My mother must make/plan/do a lot of housework every day.

Unit 05

Konglish

Travel Collocations

Right the correct collocation in the blank. There may be more than one correct answer!

1. I don't want to travel in Korea this summer, I want to travel ________________
2. She is a tour ________________ who takes groups of tourists around the city and tells them about the tourist sites.
3. I don't like ________________ tours where your hotels, food and sites are all planned before you leave. I like do things by myself!
4. For my next holiday, I want to go ________________ diving in Jeju. I hear you can see many fish and it is very exciting.
5. I was late to the airport and ________________ my flight.

Listening : Listen and fill in the missing words then answer the questions.

Many Koreans feel *(1)*__________ when they hear foreigners talk about Konglish. Others feel *(2)*__________ and enjoy using Konglish. Is Konglish bad English? Many linguists don't think so. All *(3)*__________ are always changing and evolving. People stop using some vocabulary and *(4)*__________ new words and expressions. The English used 100 years ago is very *(5)*__________ than the English we use today. And the English in the *(6)*__________ is going to be different too.

The English language has *(7)*__________ thousands of words from other languages. The definition of many words has *(8)*__________ too. Korean English is doing the same thing. As long as the words and expressions are used consistently and people who are speaking to each other *(9)*__________ what the words mean, it is not bad English, it is becoming another *(10)*__________ of English, like Singapore or Philippine English. Koreans should never feel *(11)*__________ of using Konglish.

Listening - Questions

1. How do Koreans feel about Konglish?

2. Do languages stay the same for a long time?

3. Is Konglish bad English? Why or why not?

4. What is Konglish becoming?

5. How do you feel about using Konglish?

Unit 05

Speaking : Underline the Konglish words or expressions and change them to Standard English.

1. Can I borrow your Hotchkiss? I'm giving the students handouts today.
2. She's so happy. Yesterday she had a meeting with a very handsome boy.
3. There was a scandal because the married gagman was dating the backdancer.

4. His Tico is so old. The back mirror and handle are both broken, and the tire has a punc.

5. For Christmas, the husband gave his wife a beautiful one-piece and she gave him some silk panties.

6. Tonight, I'm not feeling well so I don't want any live beer. Just give me a cider.

7. The teacher was very upset because two of his favorite students were cunning during the test.

8. The boy cut himself with a McGuyver knife.

9. He broke up with his lover yesterday and he is already planning to go to Hongdae with his friends to hunt girls tonight.

10. The bartender gave us the drinks service because my friend is very glamour.

Check your answers with your partner and then with the teacher. Now, practice the following. One student reads the Konglish sentence and the other student repeats the following.

Eg. A) Can I borrow your <u>hotchkiss</u>? I'm giving the students handouts today.

B) <u>Hotchkiss</u>? What is a <u>Hotchkiss</u>? I've never heard that word before.

A) <u>Hotchkiss</u> is a Konglish word. In Standard English, you say stapler.

Or A) His Tico is so old. The <u>back mirror</u> and handle are both broken, and the tire has a punc.

B) Back mirror, handle, punc? What are they? I've never heard those words before.

A) They are Konglish words. In Standard English you say rearview mirror, steering wheel, and flat tire.

Editing : Fix the following sentences.

1. I like to do a shower before I go to bed.
2. The pilot drives the airplane two weeks every month.
3. The casino dealer has to mix the cards before he deals them to the players.
4. My mother cooks very delicious kimbap.
5. My car won't turn on because the battery is dead.

Unit 06

Review

Unit 01 Using a Dictionary

Vocabulary

Write down the meaning of the following abbreviations.

1. Sth—
2. NZE—
3. Sing.—
4. AmE—
5. PHR V—
6. Sb—
7. Pl.—
8. BrE—

Grammar

Use the following phrasal verbs correctly in the following sentences: turn on, look forward to, pick up, try on, look at, give back.

1. That's my book. Please ______________ it ______________ to me!
2. I haven't had a vacation in a long time so I'm really ____________ it.
3. The news is going to start. Can you please ______________ the TV?
4. I need to go to the school to ______________ my son at 4p.m.
5. You should ______________ these jeans. They are so comfortable.

Dialogue

Fill in the blanks with the correct vocabulary and then practice the dialogue with a partner.

Frank: How often do you *(1)*__________ your dictionary when you study English?

Jiyeon: I'm always using it. Usually, I use an *(2)*______________ dictionary on my smart phone, but sometimes I use my father's book dictionary too.

Frank: Really? *(3)*_______ do you use that?

Jiyeon: It has so many more *(4)*______________ of words being used. I find it much easier to *(5)*__________ the words I'm studying if I can see a lot of examples.

Frank: Do you find it difficult to find idioms and phrasal *(6)*_________ in a dictionary?

Jiyeon: It depends. My father also has a learner's dictionary which is a lot more useful for ESL students than a regular dictionary.

Unit 06

Unit 02 Slang and Idioms

Vocabulary

Fill in the blanks with the correct vocabulary.

1. Someone who speaks another language perfectly is _______________ in that language.

2. A special two or three word verb that has a preposition with it is a _______________.

3. Many large countries have _______________ problems because people in the country have different cultures and customs depending on where they live.

4. That music is really ________________. My mother used to listen to it in the 1980s!

5. When you give a speech to a large group of people, you need to use ________________ and ________________ language so everyone will understand you.

Grammar

Underline the correct phrasal verb for the following sentences.

1. We are all looking forward to/looking up to graduation.
2. Look for!/Look out! There is a shark in the water!
3. I don't know what this word means so I need to look it up/into in the dictionary.
4. We are making up/for the mountain. We hope to arrive there tonight.
5. The teacher is making/looking into the cheating scandal in his class.

Dialogue

Fill in the blanks with the correct vocabulary and practice the dialogue with your partner.

Jangmi: Teacher, do you think I am *(1)*___________ my time learning slang and idioms?

Teacher: No, I don't. But I think some students *(2)*__________ too much time on slang and idioms. It's much more *(3)*__________ to spend most of your time studying more *(4)*__________ things like phrasal verbs.

Jangmi: But when I hear Junho speaking he is always using slang. It *(5)*__________ many of the students.

Teacher: It doesn't impress me. He often *(6)*__________ them and sounds silly. He wants to sound like a *(7)*__________ speaker but it's not a very *(8)*__________ goal.

Jangmi: But it's kind of cool to speak in slang.

Teacher: I know, but it's more impressive to speak so people understand you. Your English is very good Jangmi. Don't worry so much about slang and idioms!

Unit 06

Unit 03 Dialects

Vocabulary

Fill in the blanks with the correct vocabulary.

1. Korean sounds are hard for English speakers to p______________.
2. She's from China and she just moved to America, so she speaks English with a heavy Chinese a______________.
3. Britain has many r______________ dialects where people speak differently depending on where they come from.
4. The s______________ Korean dialect is the Seoul dialect. All of the news announcers speak it.
5. "말도 안돼요!" is a very c______________ Korean expression.

Unit 06 Review

Grammar

Read the sentences, underline the adverbs, and write what kind of adverb it is in the blank (manner, place, time, degree, or frequency).

1. How long has he worked there?—
2. I worked at the restaurant last night. —
3. She sometimes studies in the library. —
4. The children should sleep upstairs in the spare bedroom. —
5. My father walked quickly. —
6. The teacher speaks slowly so the students understand. —
7. The boss was angry because the workers arrived late. —
8. The taxi driver drove fast. —
9. My mother was quite pleased with her cooking. —
10. You must go home right now. —

Dialogue

Fill in the missing expressions and words in the dialogue.

Suji: Wow! You're studying hard as usual. What are you studying?

Sungmin: It's a book *(1)*__________ British English expressions.

Suji: Is British English different from American English?

Sungmin: Yes, it's a completely *(2)*__________ dialect. The pronunciation and expressions are both very different.

Suji: How are they different?

Sungmin: Well, in American English, people say *(3)*__________, but in Britain, they say mate. In America, they say, "I live in an

Apartment." But in Britain they say, "I live in a flat."

Suji: You really learn fast! Why are you studying British English?

Sungmin: Two *(4)*__________: first, I'm going for a 4 week trip to England next month. Second, I hope to work at a hotel in London next year and most of my co-workers and guests will be British.

Unit 04 Pronunciation

Vocabulary

Translate the following into English.

1. 자음—
2. 유창한—
3. 음성학—
4. 음절—
5. 발음—
6. 억양—
7. 모음—
8. 강세—

Unit 06

Grammar

Put the adverbs in the correct position in the sentences.

1. He is an interesting person. (really)
2. Are you a teacher? No. I'm a student. (actually)
3. I studied one hour for the test. (only)
4. I didn't like pizza. Really? I didn't like it. (either)
5. You like ice cream? Me. (too)

Dialogue

Fill in the missing expressions and words in the dialogue.

Junyoung: You look like your working hard. *(1)*________________?

Heeyeon: I'm studying pronunciation.

Junyoung: What is that? That doesn't look like English.

Heeyeon: It's the *(2)*__________ alphabet. I'm studying it to help me learn how to say new words I when I'm looking them up in a dictionary.

Junyoung: You think learning pronunciation will help you speak *(3)*__________ like a native speaker?

Heeyeon: No, of course not. But it will help my listening and it will also help improve my speaking.

Junyoung: I really want to speak perfectly like a *(4)*__________ speaker!

Heeyeon: That's silly. You don't need to speak perfect English to be understood and respected.

Unit 05 Konglish

Vocabulary

Fill in the blanks with the correct vocabulary.

1. English has b____________________ many words from other languages.

2. Is not -isn't, Are not -aren't. These are examples of c__________________ in English.

3. You can find a word's d__________________ in a dictionary.

4. Words that belong together like "fly······ a plane" or "write······ a letter" are examples of c__________________.

5. In English, words like "sumo" and "kimchi" are examples of b__________________ words.

Grammar

Read the sentences and underline the correct word collocation.

1. The teachers all like him because he is such a easy/hard/fun working student.
2. Wow! Look at the sunshine. It's a handsome/good-looking/beautiful day.
3. This bulgogi tastes a little bit fun/interesting/funny. Did you put too much salt in it?
4. Please open the window to get some clean/fresh/new air in the room.
5. My English class has oral/talking/speaking interviews next week with the teacher.

Unit 06

Dialogue

Fill in the blanks with the correct words and then practice the dialogue with your partner.

Michelle: Hey, do you want to go *(1)*__________ shopping with me tomorrow?

Suji: Don't you mean "window shopping?" Why are you using *(2)*__________?

Michelle: Konglish is fun. Plus everyone in Korea *(3)*__________ it, so why is it a problem?

Suji: Isn't it bad *(4)*__________?

Michelle: No. English around the world has many different *(5)*__________. This is just a Korean variety. As long as everyone understands, it shouldn't be a problem.

Suji: Who *(6)*__________ you Konglish?

Michelle: I learned from hanging out with Koreans and hearing it all the time. It was a bit *(7)*__________ to use at first, but now I love it.

Unit 07

Finding a Job

Warm-up : Skills and Strengths

Brainstorm different skills required in different jobs.

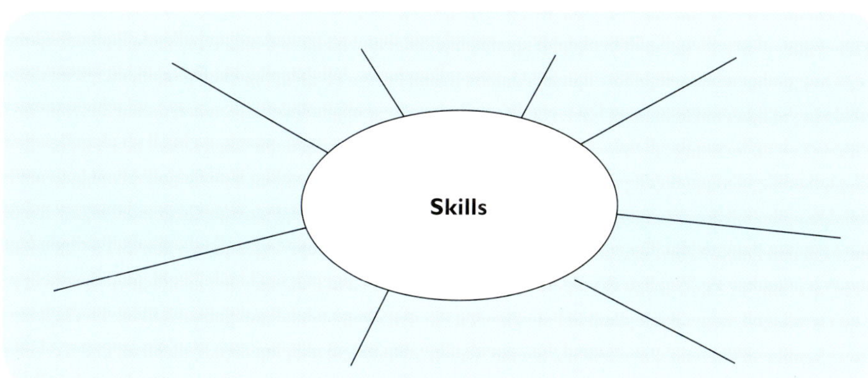

For the following jobs, write down some of the skills they need. For the last four blanks, choose any job you want to describe.

Eg. **Chef:** Chefs needs to be good at cooking.

1. Radiologist: ____________________
2. Dental Hygienist: ____________________
3. Florist: ____________________
4. Tour Conductor: ____________________

5. Physical Therapist: ______________________________

6. Nutritionist: ______________________________

7. __________: ______________________________

8. __________: ______________________________

9. __________: ______________________________

10. __________: ______________________________

Share the last four jobs by reading the skills and strengths with your partner and let your partner guess what the job is.

Vocabulary : Complete the job advertisement with the verbs from the word bank. Use the words in brackets to help you.

word Bank

communication skills	basic to intermediate	ambitious
ideal candidate	effective	resume
team player	major	growth potential
experience		

TRAVEL AGENT / CUSTOMER SERVICE REPRESENTATIVE

Job Type: Full Time | Location: Winnipeg, MB, CANADA

Number Of Positions: 6 | Salary: $30,000-49,999

The *(1)*__________ (optimal applicant) will have a solid work history combined with a strong customer service background. If you are an excellent *(2)*__________ (colleague), with strong *(3)*______________ (ability to convey information effectively), this is the position for you!!

Qualifications:

- Strong customer service orientation combined with *(4)*_______ *(efficient)* telephone and customer relationship building skills
- Excellent written and verbal communication and organizational skills
- *(5)*_________________ *(fundamental to moderate)*level computer skills: accurate and quick *(35 wpm)* keyboarding skills, Microsoft Office
- Previous industry experience in hotel reservations an asset
- *(6)*_________ *(knowledge gained from a previous encounter)* as a travel agent an asset
- Experience as a customer service representative anasset
- University degree an asset preferably a *(7)*_____ *(a study or field of study chosen by a university student)* in Tourism

If you are positive, *(8)*_______ *(eager)* and looking for a position with excellent *(9)*_________________ *(possibility for further development)*, please forward your *(10)*______ *(outline of experiences and education)*

APPLY NOW!

Dialogue : Find and underline words from the VOCABULARY section. Then, practice the dialogue with your partner.

Unit 07

Sam: What kind of job do you want after graduation?

Jen: I have no idea. But I like my major so I will be looking for a job in my field of study.

Sam: That's great. Have you done anything to prepare for employment?

Jen: Well, I have been trying to write an effective resume but it's hard.

Sam: I heard in order to be an ideal candidate, you should prove that you are a positive and ambitious team player with previous experience in the field, good communication skills, growth potential and basic to intermediate computer skills.

Jen: What? That's a lot. I thought I just needed my university degree.

Sam: Many companies say that's an asset but most applicants have their bachelor's degree.

Finding a Job

Jen: This job hunting is going to be a lot harder than I thought.

Sam: Don't worry, you will be fine. Just try to find what you love to do in life.

Grammar : Let's learn all about present perfect and its uses!

Forms	Examples	Usage Meaning
Statement: Have/has + past participle (p.p)	• I have been to Paris on a business trip. • I have presented before a board of trustees. • Mark has had many job interviews. • George has failed to get a job again.	• Present perfect is often used when the time is not mentioned: USE 1 Unspecified Time Before Now 
Contraction: Pronoun + have = 've Pronoun + has = 's	• She's just submitted her resume yesterday, but she already got the job. • I've just eaten with my co-workers.	• It is often used when the time is recent: • It is often used with ***just***
Question: Have/has + subject + past participle	• How long have you worked here? ◇ I have worked here for 10 years. *(And I'm still working here now.)* • How long has James lived in Seoul? ◇ James has lived in Seoul for 5 years. *(And he's still living here now.)*	• The present perfect is used when the time period has not finished. • Talk about actions that continue from the past to the present. • It is often used with ***for*** and ***since***. USE 2 Duration From the Past Until Now 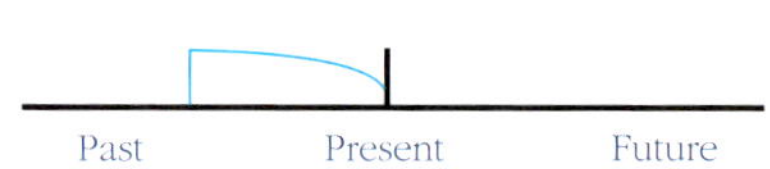

Forms	Examples	Usage Meaning
Negative: Have/has + not + past participle	• She has not sold computers since 1978. *(And she's still not selling.)* • We haven't had any news yet. • He hasn't had any experience in accounting. • Jane still hasn't finished her resume. • I've never seen the CEO.	• The adverbs ***ever, never, yet, still,*** and ***already*** are often used with the present perfect.

Complete these sentences using the present perfect form of the verbs in parenthesis and identify the usage meaning.

Eg. I have attended (attend) many job interview seminars.

Usage meaning: used because the time is not mentioned.

1. ________________ (apply) for many jobs recently.

Usage Meaning: ____

2. James________________ (go) for many job interviews since 2007.

Usage Meaning: ____

3. What ________________ (you learn) from your other jobs?

Usage Meaning: ____

4. No thank you. I________________ just (have) a cup of coffee.

Usage Meaning: ____

5. Kim ________________ (work) here for 10 years.

Usage Meaning: ____

Unit 07

Unit 07

Finding a Job

Reading : Read the job advertisements and answer the questions.

Science Teacher	Hotel Management	Dreamland Cruise Ship
Well-known Science institution seeks entry-level teacher. Must have experience with younger students, teaching degree and an outgoing personality. Salary is $38,000 a year. Call or e-mail for details.	Five-star hotel seeks hard-working college graduates. Must have customer service experience. Prefer people with management experience. Salary starts at $32,000 a year. Apply now!	A day-trip tour guide position immediately available that will allow you to travel throughout North and South America. Candidates must be enthusiastic to work with many people. For more information visit our website.

1. What are the two major factors the Science insitution is looking for in an ideal candidate?

A. solid education and friendly service

B. strong communication skills and great appearance

C. experience with younger students and an outgoing personality

D. being nice to the boss and coworkers

2. What quality does the five-star hotel prefer?

____

3. Is a university degree necessary?

____

4. When can the eligible candidate start to work as a day-trip tour guide?

____

5. What do you need to do if you want to apply for this job?

____

____

6. Do you want to apply for any of these jobs? Which job? Why or why not?

____

____

Speaking and Writing : First, fill out each box by writing down different job titles. Stand up and ask/answer the questions below to match the person with the job title you have by asking the first question. Then, ask the second question and write down their answer. The first one to get four names in a row is the winner. Every name must be different! Feel free to use the Expression Bank.

Unit 07

Question 1: What kind of job do you want after graduation?

Question 2: Have you done anything to prepare for employment?

Eg.

Dental Hygienist Name: Susan Answer: I have worked at Shingu Dental Clinic to gain experience.	Tour Guide Name: ________	Physical Therapist Name: ________	Floral Designer Name: ________

Job: ________ Name: ________ Preparation:	Job: ________ Name: ________ Preparation:	Job: ________ Name: ________ Preparation:	Job: ________ Name: ________ Preparation:

Job: ______________ Name: ______________ Preparation:	Job: ______________ Name: ______________ Preparation:	Job: ______________ Name: ______________ Preparation:	Job: ______________ Name: ______________ Preparation:
Job: ______________ Name: ______________ Preparation:	Job: ______________ Name: ______________ Preparation:	Job: ______________ Name: ______________ Preparation:	Job: ______________ Name: ______________ Preparation:
Job: ______________ Name: ______________ Preparation:	Job: ______________ Name: ______________ Preparation:	Job: ______________ Name: ______________ Preparation:	Job: ______________ Name: ______________ Preparation:

Expression Bank :

gained job experience
achieved certificates
strong organizational skills
excellent time management skills
excellent oral and written communication skills
able to speak clearly and persuasively
team player
great leadership

Editing : Correct the following sentences using what you have learned in this unit.

1. She have not read the e-mail yet.

____

2. I have not never been on a business trip.

____

3. Had Karl had a job interview at CJ Corporation yet?

____

4. We've still not ate our dinner.

____

5. They's already chosen someone for the position.

____

Unit 07

Unit 08

Resume and Interview

Warm-up : Let's compare and contrast the following two resumes.

(입사) 지원서

반명함판 (3cm x 4cm)	성명	한 글		생 년 월 일	(남 · 여)
		한 자		주민등록번호	
	E - mail			휴대전화	
	주 소				(TEL.)

학력	기 간	학 교 명	전 공 분 야
	~	초등학교(졸 · 중퇴)	
	~	중 학 교(졸 · 중퇴)	
	~	고등학교(졸 · 중퇴)	
	~	대 학 교(졸 · 중퇴)	
	~	대 학 원(졸 · 중퇴)	

경력	기 간	근 무 처	직 위	업 무 내 용
	~			
	~			

자격및 면허	자 격 · 면 허 명	시 행 처		취 득 년 월 일
	. . .			
	. . .			
	. . .			

어학	언 어	시 험 명	등급/점수	취 득 년 월 일
				. . .
				. . .

병역	복 무 기 간	군 별	계 급	병 과	미 필 또 는 면 제 사 유
	~				

신장	cm	체중	kg	혈액형		취 미		종 교	

경력사항	관 계	성 명	연 령	출 신 학 교	직 업	근 무 처	직 위

Resume

- Your name
- Home address
- Contact Number
- Email address

Objective Statement

- express why you want this employment and show you are an ideal candidate for this job

Summary of Qualifications

- Foreign language
- Typing speed
- Computer/Software
- any other skills that "fit" the specific job description

Education (list all relevant education)

- Degrees (highest 1st)
- Certifications
- Training

Work Experience

- list your work history chronologically
- Name of the company, the dates of employment, and your position should be included
- Briefly describe your responsibilities / achievements

Activities & Associations

- Organizations
- Associations
- Student government
- Community activities

References Available Upon Request

How are the two resumes similar? How are the two resumes different? List attributes on the chart in the two areas indicated.

Similar	Different

Vocabulary : Match the following words to their Korean definitions. Then, underline the words in the resume and see how they were used.

Unit 08

1. Qualifications	**a.** 책임
2. Responsibilities	**b.** 전문학사학위
3. Objective	**c.** 업적, 성취
4. Associate Degree	**d.** 종업원
5. Effectively	**e.** 증빙서류
6. Committed	**f.** 직무능력개발
7. Co-workers	**g.** 효율적으로
8. Professional Development	**h.** 헌신적인, 열성적인
9. Achievements	**i.** (4년제) 학사학위
10. Employee	**j.** 목적
11. Bachelor's Degree	**k.** 동료
12. References	**l.** 자격

Julie Moon

010.1234.5678 juliemoon@naver.com

PROFESSIONAL OBJECTIVE

To gain valuable work experience and become a physical therapist in order to apply my knowledge and continue to grow with the company and keep learning by taking on more responsibilities.

EDUCATION

Associate Degree of Physical Therapy, Shingu University, Sungnam (Feb. 2010-Feb. 2012)

SUMMARY OF QUALIFICATIONS

- Work effectively with diverse groups of people
- A friendly, competent and hardworking employee and good relationships with co-workers
- Committed to professional development
- Excellent interpersonal and oral and written communications skills in English and Korean
- Type speed: 55wpm. Korean type speed: 120cpm (characters per minute)

PROFESSIONAL EXPERIENCE

Waitress and Customer Support Agent

Firenze, Moran, Korea

February 2009 to Present

Controlled and balanced daily bookings and reservations. Trained staff concerning computerized reservation system. Inputted customer requirements and information.

Cashier

Burger King, Seoul

March 2007 to March 2008

Maintained clean and friendly environment, assisted customers, and was responsible with finance

AWARDS AND ACHIEVEMENTS

Scholarship: Department Scholarship ($500), 2008

Certifications : Microsoft Office, 2009

Volunteer: Retirement Home and Disabled Children's House, 2010-2011

♣ References Available Upon Request ♣

Dialogue : **Read the following dialogue and answer the following questions. Find and underline words from the VOCABULARY section.**

Interviewer: Ms Moon, welcome to Shingu Hospital. Why do you want to work for us?

Ms. Moon: My professional objective is to become a great physical therapist at a place where I can apply my skills and further develop my experience and knowledge. I know Shingu Hospital will give me that opportunity.

Interviewer: Thank you. Could you tell us what qualifications you have that will help you while working at our hospital?

Ms. Moon: I have many qualifications although I do not have any professional experiences in this field. As stated under awards and achievements, I volunteered at a retirementhome and disabled children's house. Because I have an associate degree in Physical Therapy, I used what I learned at school and helped the elderly and disabled children with their mobility. In addition, I work effectively, so I am able to complete any given task quickly and accurately. Also, wherever I've worked, I have always had a great relationship with my co-workers.

Interviewer: Lastly, what will you do if you get hired?

Ms. Moon: I will take my responsibilities seriously and become a valuable employee who will put forth the best effort. Also, I will continue to grow by being committed to professional development.

1. Why did Ms. Moon choose Shingu Hospital?

____

____

2. What did Ms. Moon do at her volunteer place?

____

____

3. Do you think Shingu Hospital will hire Ms. Moon? Why or why not?

____

____

Grammar : Let's learn all about the passive and its uses!

Active Sentence:	Samsung	hired	10 new employees.
	(Subject)	(Verb)	(Object)
Passive Sentence:	10 new employees	were hired	by Samsung.
	(Subject)	(Verb)	(Object)

From of the Passive
BE+Past Participle

1. Both sentences have the same meaning.

2. The object in an active sentence becomes the subject in a passive sentence.

3. The subject in an active sentence is the object of "**by**" in a passive sentence. In this case, the focus is on the subject of a sentence rather than the person who performs the action.

Eg. The questions are asked by the interviewers.
(The focus of attention is on the questions.)

The decisions were made by the CEO.

(The focus of attention is on the decisions.)

4. The passive is usually used without a "**by-phrase**." This is because the passive is mainly used when the information on who performs an action is unknown.

Eg. The job offers were made to the interviewees who answered with confidence.

(It is not known or important to know exactly who made the job offers.)

James was promoted to general manager.

(It is not known or important to know exactly who promoted James.)

Let's practice what you have learned.

Unit 08

A. Change the active sentences to passives that have the same meaning.

1. The news excited Matt.

____

2. Did the news excite his parents?

____

3. Sunny signed the employment contract.

____

4. Did the CEO ask you to sign the contract, too?

____

5. The secretary faxed the acceptance letter to newly hired employees.

____

B. Complete the sentences with the passive form of the verbs in parentheses.

My first job as a radiologist

I *(1)*________________________ (hire) by Shingu hospital after I graduated from Shingu University. The excitement of getting a job at this hospital *(2)*________________________ (shared) by many people including my parents. However, I *(3)*________________________ (burden) by many responsibilities I had to perform:senior radiologists *(4)*________________________ (assist) with specialized procedures, reports *(5)*________________________ (give) to the radiologists for each patient, general ultrasound *(6)*________________________ (performed), unusual or inconsistent findings *(7)*________________________ (report) to senior radiologists, etc. In spite of all these duties, I kept working hard because great pride *(8)*________________________ (give) to my parents.

Listening : Listen to the following script and fill in the blanks. Then, evaluate each answer as poor, good, or excellent and justify your evaluation.

Be prepared to share your reasons with the class.

1. How would you *(1)* ________________ ?

I majored in Tax Accounting from Shingu University. I don't like my major but my parents wanted me to become an accountant. I am obedient, so now I'm applying for this position. *(2)* ____________ my parents will be very happy.

Poor / Good / Excellent : (Give reason for your evaluation)

____

2. **What specific** *(3)* ________ **have you** *(4)* __________ **for your life?**

I am *(5)* ___________ person. I work really hard to *(6)* __________.
So, I have always achieved the goals I have set. More importantly, I *(7)* ________________ carefully and realistically. For example, I set a goal to graduate with good grades, and I graduated top of my class.

Poor / Good / Excellent : (Give reason for your evaluation)

____

3. **How has your** *(8)* _____________ **prepared you for** *(9)* _________?

Sorry, I am not prepared because I've never had a job. I just wanted to *(10)* _________ on my studies, so I didn't even have a *(11)* _____________.

Poor / Good / Excellent : (Give reason for your evaluation)

____

4. **What** *(12)* ___________ **you to choose** *(13)* ___________?

My *(14)* _____________ have shown me that I enjoy serving others. I really love helping others. When people I helped are happy, it makes me feel important. That's why I have chosen this career.

Poor / Good / Excellent : (Give reason for your evaluation)

____

Unit 08

5. **Why should we *(15)* __________ you?**

I should be hired because I am *(16)* __________ and ready to do whatever you want me to do. I will *(17)* __________________ to be one of the most *(18)* _____________ and proud employees of this company.

Poor / Good / Excellent : (Give reason for your evaluation)

____

Speaking and Writing : Use today's DIALOGUES and LISTENING section as a guide.

1. Work in groups of six.
2. Divide the group into two: 3 interviewers and 3 interviewees.
3. Your teacher will give each of you a resume. Do NOT show your resume to anyone.
4. By using the resume given to you, interviewers ask 3 job interview questions to interviewees.
5. By using the resume given to you, interviewees answer the questions.
6. Once everyone had a turn in asking and answering questions, find your ideal employer/employee. You should have the same resume.

Here are some useful expressions you can use.

Category	Interviewer	Interviewee
Experience	What did you learn from your last job/school?	I learned to··· I had a problem with···.
	What were your responsibilities at your last job?	My responsibilities were ··· I didn't have much responsibilities···
Skills	What are your strengths and weaknesses?	My strengths are··· My weaknesses are···
	Do you have any special skills?	I am good at···
Future Plans	What do you want to do in the future?	My aim is to ··· I plan to···
	What do you want to accomplish?	I want to accomplish···
About you	Please describe your work style.	I spend a lot of time··· I like to··· I don't like to···
	What are you passionate about?	I am passionate about···

Editing : Correct the following mistakes using what you have learned in this unit.

1. The students was taught to write a good resume.

   ____

2. John was interview by the manager.

   ____

3. Where are the job advertisements post in the bulletin boards?

   ____

4. The dinner were served to newly hired employees.

   ____

5. The welcoming speech was gave by the CEO of the company.

   ____

Unit 09

Taking Instructions On The Job

Warm-up : Work with a partner and decide which word goes best with each verb.

1. Book

a) a conference

b) a room

c) a business

d) an incident

2. Set up

a) a cigarette

b) a mail

c) a meeting

d) a light switch

3. Make

a) an appointment

b) a room

c) an incident

d) an accident

4. Open

a) a switch

b) a demand

c) an incident

d) a new branch

5. Take on

a) a shirt

b) a new employee

c) an accident

d) a room

Vocabulary

book	take on	open
make	set up	perks
consensus	minutes	point out
summary	deadline	interrupt
in a jiffy	regarding	referring
as well	takeover	zero tolerance policy
24-7	delay	

Unit 09

Vocabulary exercises : Choose words from the vocabulary list above to fit the definitions listed below.

1. ______________________ : to be available at all hours of the day, all days of the week

2. ______________________ : a record of things discussed in a meeting

3. ______________________ : to do something very quickly

4. ____________________: special privileges or benefits

5. ____________________: to arrange a meeting

6. ____________________: to reserve a space or a time

7. ____________________: an agreement between two or more people or parties

8. ____________________: to bring attention to something

9. ____________________: in addition

10. ____________________: a condition where something is absolutely unacceptable

Dialogue : A Dastardly Day

Mr. Jerk: Hee-jeong, I need you to book me a room at my favorite hotel in Kansas City.

Hee-jeong: I'm sorry sir, but I don't know which hotel you mean.

Mr. Jerk: I'm *(1)* ______________ to the hotel that is located downtown. I stayed there last week when I flew in for that business *(2)* ______________.

Hee-jeong: Are you referring to the Hamilton Hotel, sir?

Mr. Jerk: Yes, that's the one, and could you *(3)* ______________ a meeting with Mrs. Howl aswell? Make the appointment for Tuesday afternoon. I need to reach a *(4)* __________ with her regarding the new branch we plan to open.

Hee-jeong: Yes sir, but which Mrs. Howl are you referring to? There are three Mrs. Howls listed in your address book.

Mr. Jerk: I am referring to the one whom I had dinner with last Thursday. The woman who goes by the name of Ginger Howl, the woman whom…

Hee-jeong: Ginger Howl. Yes sir, I've got it.

Mr. Jerk: Don't *(5)* _______________ me dear. If you do that again I'll have you replaced in a jiffy.

Hee-jeong: Yes, sir. I'm sorry to have interrupted you.

Mr. Jerk: That's a good girl. You're catching on. Keep doing a good job and there may be some extra *(6)* _______________ for you in the future.

Hee-jeong: Where do you plan on meeting Mrs. Howl?

Mr. Jerk: Now hold on dear. You're interrupting again. Do you remember what happened to the last secretary who interrupted me?

Hee-jeong: Yes sir, I did hear about the last secretary who interrupted you. That was the woman who recently quit and filed a complaint about you.

Mr. Jerk: Well then, um, yes- be a good girl and give me a summary of what I've just told you.

Hee-jeong: You told me to *(7)* _______________ you a room in your favorite hotel in Kansas City that is located downtown. Then you told me to set up an appointment with Mrs. Ginger Howl.

Mr. Jerk: Exactly my dear. Now be a good sweetie and massage my shoulders.

Hee-jeong: I'm sorry sir, but massages were not mentioned in the job advertisement that you posted *(8)* _______________ a new secretary.

Taking Instructions On The Job

Grammar (Relative Clauses) : We use relative clauses to give additional information without using more than one sentence. To do this we include relative pronouns.

who, whom, whose

who	"Who" is a subject pronoun that replaces "he", "she", "we", etc. It refers to the person that does something or to the people that do something.
whom	"Whom" is an object pronoun that replaces "him", "her", "us", etc. It refers to the person that receives an action or to the people that receive an action.
whose	"Whose" is a possessive pronoun that replaces "his", "her", "our", etc. It refers to which person something belongs to.

See the examples below:

relative pronoun	intended information	relative clause
who	A student cheated on the exam. I told you about him.	I told you about the student **who** cheated on the exam.
whom	You told me about the pastor. I met him.	I met the pastor whom you told me about.
whose	I met the singer. Her father was dumb.	I met the singer **whose** father was dumb.

that, which

that	The word "that" is used to introduce information that cannot be omitted without altering the meaning of a sentence.
which	The word "which" is used to introduce extra information that can be removed without changing the meaning of the sentence. This information is set apart with commas.

See the examples below:

relative pronoun	intended information	relative clause
that	It's important to eat food. It is essential that this food be nutritious.	It's important to eat food that is nutritious.
which	It's important to eat nutritious food. If it tastes good then that is good too.	Eating nutritious food, which happens to be tasty as well, is important.

Grammar exercises : Fill in the blanks with the correct relative pronouns.

1. Did you meet the woman ______________ I told you about?
2. Mr. Park is the man ______________ father was elected president of our company.
3. Suzie Rhee is the girl ______________ practices faith healing on animals.
4. Could you please repair the clock ______________ I told you about?
5. Tiffany liked the expensive bracelet, ______________ was made of diamonds.
6. Sheila is looking for a man ______________ makes a lot of money.
7. Dale is looking for a woman ______________ parents are rich.
8. The police are looking for the thief ______________ stole Tiffany's bracelet.
9. Students want jobs ______________ pay well.
10. Nobody likes people ______________ blow their noses without using tissue.

Unit 09

Taking Instructions On The Job

Reading : The Advice Column

Read and identify as many relative clauses as you can.

Dear Lanny,

I am having trouble following my director's instructions and I don't know what to do. He refers to me in condescending terms such as "dear", "honey", and "sweetie" when asking me to take memos or minutes of meetings that are held in his office. He insists that I stay in the office late at night when all of the other employees, whom happen to be male, are free to leave and go home. He places my chair very close to his and asks me to sit down in it. I don't like sitting in a chair that is placed so close to him. Sometimes he touches my hair or my hand and tells me that I'm beautiful. He told me that I needed to be available for him 24-7 because we have deadlines that must be met. Why is it only me who has to stay late? I want to ask him that, but I'm afraid that I'll lose my job if I complain.

Just yesterday he asked me to book a hotel room for his Kansas City trip and he suggested that I join him. I refused, but he said there would be extra perks for a good secretary who did everything he asked. It has become unbearable. I never thought I'd have a job that felt like such a torture. I've talked to friends whose bosses don't act like mine and they tell me to quit and find a new job, but the economy is so bad and jobs are hard to find. What should I do?

Yours sincerely,

Abused and Confused Hee-jeong

Dear Abused and Confused Hee-jeong,

You should know that what you are experiencing is sexual harassment. It is defined as unwanted or offensive sexual behavior toward a colleague based on their gender and includes spoken remarks as well as uninvited physical contact. Sexual harassment is illegal in most countries. Workplaces in these countries have adopted a zero tolerance policy in regard to it.

For example, colleges that discourage sexual harassment require their professors to attend sexual harassment seminars. These seminars teach that professors who touch their students inappropriately and teachers who try to date or marry their students are engaging in improper behavior. Seminars that address sexual harassment also emphasize that it is usually initiated by someone in a position of authority who directs their improper behavior toward someone who has less power

Of course colleges are not the only workplace where sexual harassment can exist. It exists in company offices, hospitals, laboratories, and in the service industry as well. The real question for anyone who feels harrassed is what to do about it.

Speakers who give seminars on sexual harassment suggest that the person who feels harassed should, first of all, approach the offender face to face and express their disapproval of the behavior that has taken place. Then, if the person who has committed the offense does not change this behavior, the person who feels sexually harassed should make their complaint to a higher authority.

My advice to you is to simply tell your boss how you feel. Let him know that you don't approve and then see what happens. If he doesn't change his ways then talk to someone else about it. It is a problem which is increasingly debated and which many workplaces are taking measures to reduce.

Yours sincerely,

Lanny

Taking Instructions On The Job

Comprehension : Look back through the article and find the answers to the following questions.

1. How often does Hee-jeong's boss expect her to be available?
2. What are three things he does that make her feel uncomfortable?
3. What does Lanny call this problem?
4. What policies do many workplaces have in regard to this problem?
5. What are three kinds of workplaces where this problem occurs?

Discussion : Do you agree with the instructive advice Lanny gave Hee-jeong? Talk with your partner and write a reply to Hee-jeong with your own instruction.

Dear Abused and Confused Hee-jeong,

____

____

____

____

____

____

____

____

____

yours sincerely,

____________________ and ____________________ .

Editing : Correct the following sentences.

1. I want to talk to the person which is in charge.

2. I saw the doctor whose you told me about.

3. Did you find the dog whom you lost?

4. I ran a marathon, that was my third full-length marathon, last week.

5. Is he the boy who parents won the lottery?

Unit 09

Unit 10

Problems at Work

Warm-up : Look at following problems. Which problems are work related and which are school related? Put the problems in the correct column and number them from worst to best. Try to think of a few more problems. Some problems can go in both columns. Compare your problems to your partners and then check them together as a class.

Problems :

Sexual Harassment	Too much homework	Finish too late
A member of your team is lazy	Noisy classmates	Your team leader makes youdrink soju.
Very low pay	Must study for TOIEC test	Cubicle is too small
Only one or two weeks of vacation every year.	Physical abuse	Computer viruse
Must pass test for promotion		Need good grades for scholarship
Must be polite to rude customers		Seniors make you drink at MTs

Work Problems | School Problems

Vocabulary : Match the following words and expressions with their synonyms.

1. Job benefits ___
2. Good points and bad points ___
3. Sick and tired ___
4. Bother ___
5. Salary ___
6. Rude ___
7. Promotion ___
8. Overwork ___
9. Quit the job ___
10. Current ___

a. dislike very much
b. pay
c. leave the company
d. annoy
e. perks
f. increase in pay and responsibilities
g. nowadays
h. impolite
i. pros and cons
j. work long hours

Unit 10

Use the above vocabulary and expressions to complete the following sentences.

1. I'm really ______________________ of all the overtime at my job. I never get to see my family and friends anymore.
2. I've been married three times and my ______________ wife wants to divorce me because I'm always at work.
3. I get a lot of ______________ working at the Hilton. I can stay in any Hilton around the world for free and get discounts on all the restaurants.

4. There are many ______________ about working as a pilot. I get to travel all around the world but my family misses me and I don't work regular hours.

5. I just got a big ______________! I have to work a little more but my salary is much bigger.

6. My boss is never ______________ to me or my coworkers so everyone respects him.

Dialogue 1 : **Read the dialogue and answer the questions. Check the answers with your partner and then with your teacher. Then read the dialogue together with your partner.**

Eunmi: Hey John, how are things going at work these days?

John: Not so good. I'm already really busy working on the new training program for new employees but my manager stopped by today and asked me if I could plan the business trip to Bangkok for next month.

Eunmi: It sounds like he overworks you.

John: He sure does. I love my job, but I'm getting sick and tired of the heavy workload. These days, I start work at 7a.m. and don't leave the office until 10p.m.

Eunmi: When do you have time to meet your girlfriend?

John: Girlfriend? We broke up last month. She said it was impossible to develop a good relationship when we were only meeting once or twice a month.

Eunmi: If I were you, I'd try talking to your boss.

John: If you knew my boss, you wouldn't. He's very traditional and works even longer hours than me.

Eunmi: There must be something you like about your job. You've been working there for over five years. If there wasn't, you would have quit a long time ago.

John: Of course! I love the work I do and most of my coworkers. I also get a nice salary.

1. What problems does John have at his job these days?

2. What advice does Eunmi give him?

3. Is John's boss bad? Why or why not?

4. Is John a new employee?

5. Is John thinking about quitting his job?

Unit 10

Dialogue 2 : Answer the pre-dialogue questions and then read the dialogue to see if your answers are similar. Then answer the post-reading questions, check your answers with a partner and the class, then read the dialogue with two other students.

1. What problems do you think flight attendants have with their jobs?

2. What are some of the job perks flight attendants get?

Unit 10 Problems at Work

Jenny: Tyler, this is my good friend Areum. She's a flight attendant for Singapore Airlines.

Tyler: Wow! I love Singapore Airlines. Their customer service is so good. What's it like to work for them?

Areum: They are a very good company but being a flight attendant is a lot harder than people think.

Jenny: Really? What do you mean?

Areum: Well, the passengers can be very rude.

Tyler: How so? Give us a few examplcs, please!

Areum: A lot of passengers never listen. As soon as we land, if we tell them to keep their seatbelt fastened and to remain in their seats, a lot of the older men jump out of their seats and start taking their carry-on bags out of the overhead compartments.

Jenny: I've seen that. Any other good stories?

Areum: If passengers want something, most never say please or thank you. Just gimme gimme gimme. Or they don't even say anything, they just grab the flight attendants as they pass by.

Tyler: What about drunk passengers?

Areum: Drunk passengers are super annoying. They bother other passengers and sometimes even sexually harass flight attendants.

Jenny: But there must be a lot of perks. You don't plan on quitting anytime soon, do you?

Areum: Of course! First, we get to see a lot of wonderful cities and stay at the best hotels and it's all paid for. I also work with some really interesting people and a lot of passengers are really nice. I've met many famous singers and actors too! My family also gets a couple of free tickets every year.

Jenny: Wow. I really envy you. If I was taller, I'd be a flight attendant too.

Tyler: Yeah, it's too bad you're only 145cm!

Jenny: Shut up!

1. What is Areum's biggest complaint about working as a flight attendant?

2. Does she want to quit her job?

3. How are some passengers rude?

4. What do drunk passengers do that really annoys her?

5. Why can't Jenny be a flight attendant?

Unit 10

Grammar : "If" Conditionals-"If" introduces something that may or may not happen depending on events. There are 4 main types of conditionals: Present, 1st, 2nd, and 3rd conditionals.

Present IF + PRESENT SIMPLE + PRESENT SIMPLE

Eg. If I drink soju, I get drunk.

This means the condition can be true at any time. "If" can be replaced by "When" and the meaning is the same.

Unit 10 Problems at Work

1st conditional IF + PRESENT SIMPLE + WILL/WON'T

Eg. If it rains, I'll stay at home.

This predicts a probable future result.

2nd conditional IF + PAST SIMPLE + WOULD

Eg. If I was rich, I'd buy a sports car.

This is for imaginary events that aren't possible now or are impossible.

3rd conditional IF + PAST PERFECT + WOULD HAVE

Eg. If I had studied harder in high school, I'd have gone to Seoul National University.

Practice 1 : Fill in the blanks with PRESENT TENSE verbs, WILL, WON'T, WOULD, WOULDN'T or PRESENT PERFECT verbs.

1. If the salary is high, workers _______________ always happy.
2. If my new boss is kind, I _______________ be happy.
3. If my last boss had been kind, I would _______________ happy.
4. If I have to work overtime tonight, I _______________ go out drinking with my friends.
5. If he was a little smarter, he _______________ get a promotion.
6. If coworkers are lazy, they _______________ not popular.
7. If I hadn't gotten a job as a doctor, I would _______________ a pilot.

8. In Asia, if flight attendants get married, they usually _______________ their jobs.

9. If you work at Samsung, you _______________ need to speak some English.

10. At our hotel, if workers are rude to customers, they _______________ always fired immediately.

Practice 2 : Match the following conditionals and practice them with a partner.

1. If I had known how stressful the job was, _____
2. If I finish work early, _____
3. If my coworker is rude and mean to me, _____
4. If they ask me to work overtime tonight, _____
5. If my lazy coworker gets a raise and I don't, _____
6. If the customer hadn't been rude, _____
7. If they don't pay for overtime, _____
8. If the company doesn't treat its employees well, _____
9. If I had studied English harder in school, _____
10. If my office was bigger, _____

a. I'll be angry.

b. I'd be more comfortable and work harder.

c. I wouldn't have punched him and gotten fired.

d. many will leave the company and find work somewhere else.

e. I would have gotten a better job.

f. I wouldn't have started working here.

g. I'll say that it's my father's 60th birthday and I have to attend.

h. I'll meet my friends and go drinking.

i. I'll report it to my boss.

j. I'll complain to my boss and maybe quit.

Unit 10

Problems at Work

Listening : Listen to the three people talk about their jobs and answer the questions about each person.

Megumi Yamaguchi

1. What is her job and where does she work?

2. What are the pros and cons of her job?

Darren McDonald

1. What is his job and where does he work?

2. What do his customers like to do?

3. What is the only thing he doesn't like about his job?

4. Where can he meet his friends?

Sarah Anderson

1. What is her job?

2. What are the pros and cons of her job?

3. Why is she thinking about quiting?

Unit 11

E-mail Writing

Warm-up : When people write e-mails and use the internet, they use a lot of slang, abbreviations, and acronyms.

"Lol" means Laugh-out-loud and is used in phone texts, chatting, and in e-mails.

Unit 11

Look at the following expressions. In groups of 2 or 3, try to guess their meanings. First try without using your smart phone. After 5 minutes, you can use smart phones.

1. B4—

2. FYI—

3. FAQ—

4. EZ—

5. IMO—

6. OMG!—

7. PLZ!—

8. ASL—

9. ATTN—

10. CYA—

Unit 11 E-mail Writing

With your group, think of five more English internet slang words or expressions. Then check with another group to see if they can guess the meanings.

1.
2.
3.
4.
5.

Vocabulary : Look at the following words and translate them into Korean using your dictionaries, then complete the following sentences using the words.

professiona	personal	informal	punctuation	typo
impression	slang	emoticons	weird	contact information

1. In e-mails and text messages, ________________ of faces expressing different feelings are very popular.
2. A ________________ is a kind of spelling mistake that a person makes when they are typing too quickly and don't notice they've made a mistake.
3. If you ask an American woman how old she is when you first meet her, she thinks the question is too ________________.
4. If you don't dress nicely for the job interview, you won't give the

company a good ______________ of yourself.

5. You must write down some ______________ like your phone number or e-mail address.

6. Internet English has lots of ______________ like FYI, lol, and u2!

7. If you use too much slang and have too many spelling mistakes in a business e-mail, it isn't very ______________.

8. ______________ is just as important as spelling when writing a good e-mail.

9. He never laughs at any jokes and often talks to himself. He's very ______________.

10. The meeting is very ______________ so you don't have to wear a suit.

Unit 11

Dialogue 1 : Fill in the blanks with the following words: weekend, strange, jackets, professional, spelling, questions, terrible.

Then answer the questions about the dialogue and practice the dialogue with a partner.

Jack: This is *(1)*______________!

Wonju: What's wrong?

Jack: I sent an e-mail to a clothing company in China last week to ask them about ordering 10,000 *(2)*______________ for our company. I got the reply today.

Wonju: And?

Jack: First, the guy asks me how my *(3)*______________ was. I don't even know him and he's asking about my weekend?

Wonju: Yeah, that's really strange.

Jack: And then it's filled with tons of *(4)*______________ mistakes, punctuation mistakes, and emoticons. God! I hate those smiling faces even in personal e-mails. I can't believe it was written by someone with a university education.

Wonju: What about the jackets?

Jack: At the end of the e-mail he finally answered my *(5)*____________, but I'm not sure I want to use this company now. It just seems so weird.

Wonju: Yes, it wasn't very *(6)*______________________________

1. How does Jack feel about the e-mail?

2. What were some problems with the e-mail?

3. What does Wonju feel about the Chinese e-mail writer?

Dialogue 2 : Fill in the blanks with the following words: wordy, punctuation, depends, personal, impression, concise, title.
Then answer the questions about the dialogue and practice the dialogue with a partner.

Joe: What are you doing?

Sookjin: I'm writing a business e-mail.

Joe: What's the difference between a business e-mail and a personal one?

Sookjin: Well, first of all, a business e-mail should be clear and *(1)*_______________. If it's too long and *(2)*_______________, the reader will be put off.

Joe: Anything else?

Sookjin: Spelling and *(3)*_______________ are very important. If you don't want to give a bad *(4)*_______________, make sure you read it again before you send it. Always use spell check to fix typos!

Joe: Should I include contact information?

Sookjin: Of course you don't need to give them your e-mail address- it's included in the mail. But you should leave your name, job *(5)*_______________, and phone number at the end of your e-mail.

Joe: It definitely shouldn't be too *(6)*_______________?

Sookjin: It *(7)*_______________ on how well you know the person you're writing to. If you know them well, you can add a few personal comments, but if you don't know them well you should keep it formal.

Unit 11

1. Are there any differences between business and personal e-mails?

2. What should you include at the end of a business e-mail?

3. Is it never a good idea to be personal in a business e-mail?

4. What is one thing you don't need to give in a business e-mail?

Unit 11

E-mail Writing

Grammar

Punctuation Marks

Match the following punctuation marks with their correct name.

1. , __
2. : __
3. . __
4. ! __
5. (…………) __
6. ; __
7. "……" or '……'
8. ?__

a. period
b. semi-colon
c. parenthesis
d. exclamation point
e. question mark
f. comma
g. colon
h. quotation marks

Punctuation Problems

Commas,

1. Use commas to separate elements in a series.

Eg. I am studying English, Japanese, and Chinese. My family includes my parents, my older sister, and my younger brother.

2. Use commas with conjunctions (and, or, but, so……) to separate independent clauses.

Eg. I am studying English, but my brother is studying Japanese. She doesn't love him, so she isn't going to marry him.

3. Use commas for introductory phrases.

Eg. During my last vacation, I went to Japan. In conclusion, I really enjoyed the movie.

Colons:

1. Use colons after a sentence to introduce a list.

Eg. I need to go shopping for the following items: a notebook, some pens, an eraser, and a calculator. When my brother went to Europe, he visited the following countries: England, France, Spain, Italy, and Greece.

2. Colons are often used at the start of a business letter when addressing someone by their name instead of a comma.

Eg. Dear Mr Johnson:

Unit 11

Semi-Colons;

1. Use semi-colons in a list when parts of the list contain commas.

Eg. There are many ways to contact him; you can use a phone to call or text message, which is probably the easiest way; you can e-mail or message him on your computer; or you can go visit him in his office, but he might not be in.

2. Semi-colons are used to link two independent clauses together which are closely related in thought.

Eg. Some students use pens; others use pencils. I ate lunch at the Shingu cafeteria today; it tasted terrible.

Unit 11 E-mail Writing

Quotation Marks

1. Periods and commas always go inside quotation marks.

Eg. "I'm not sure what I'll do" he said, "but maybe I'll go for a drink."

2. Sometimes question marks go inside the quotation marks and sometimes they don't. If the person speaking in the quote is asking a question, it goes inside the quotation. If the writer is asking a question, then it goes outside the quotation. If both the writer and speaker are asking a question, then you only use one question mark and it goes inside the quotation.

Eg. She asked, "Is he coming to work today?" OR did she say, "He is really handsome"? OR did she say, "Is he handsome?"

3. Use single quotation marks for quotes inside quotes.

Eg. He said, "I heard the teacher said, He's a nice kid but a terrible student."

Practice : Put commas in the correct place in the following sentences.

1. I don't like working overtime but sometimes you have to do it.
2. In her free time my mother enjoys cooking, reading and watching movies.
3. For my next test I won't be able to study as much but I will pass it.
4. My boyfriend his sister and I went to Namdaemun market last night.
5. I didn't eat anything but I have a stomachache.

Put colons and semi-colons in the correct place in the following sentences.

1. My father enjoys any of the following things jogging, hiking, drinking with his friends, and playing go-stop.
2. He gets upset when people ask him about his age he is very sensitive.
3. On my last trip to Europe, I visited the following places London, England Paris, France and Rome, Italy.
4. Korean high school students study 24 hours a day they never get any sleep.
5. My mother is the glue that keeps our family together without her we'd break apart.

Put double or single quotation marks in the correct place in the following sentences.

Unit 11

1. My girlfriend asked me Are you going to marry me?
2. I heard my boss talking. He said, If it's not broke, don't fix it.
3. Look, he said she told me I don't love you, and she also said, I never want to see you again.
4. Oh no! he cried, I left my bag on the subway.
5. Einstein said God does not play with dice.

Unit 11 E-mail Writing

Reading : In pairs, read the following business e-mail and rewrite it using the formal expressions from the vocabulary exercise to make them less personal.

Dear John,

How are you these days? I heard you are married and have two children, so I hope you and your family are all happy and healthy. Because it's winter, you should also take care not to catch a cold!

I'm really sorry I didn't write you back sooner but my wife has been sick and I've been very busy at work. Anyways, in your e-mail, you asked us some questions. Here are the answers!

What winter clothes do we sell? We specialize in ski clothing including jackets, pants, gloves, scarves, and hats.

How long would it take for a large shipment to be delivered? We guarantee delivery in less than 4 working days.

Do we give bulk discounts? For orders of more than 5000 units, we give 7% off and for orders of 10,000 or more, we give 12% off.

If you have any more questions, please feel free to ask.

Speaking : Formal vs. Informal E-mail Expressions

Match the following informal words and expressions with the formal words and expressions with the same meaning and check your answers with a partner and then the teacher.

1. Hello friend! ___

2. Talking about the······ ___

3. Thanks for ___

4. I'm really angry about······ ___

5. I heard the news about······ ___

6. Take care and see you soon······ ___

a. Sincerely,

b. It has come to my attention that······

c. Regarding

d. I would appreciate it if······

e. To whom it may concern,

f. I was disappointed...

With another student, practice the above expressions using the following sentences. One student reads from the book and the other student closes their book and practices answering from memory.

Unit 11

A: I'm writing a business e-mail. Does "Hello friend!" sound too informal?

B: Yes, it would sound better if you wrote, "To whom it may concern."

Complete the following e-mail using the above expressions.

*(1)*____ ,

I am writing *(2)*________________________ a picture on your company's website. *(3)*________________________ used a picture of some children in a playground. One of the children is my daughter. *(4)*________________________ that you used this picture without my permission.

*(5)*______________________________________ you changed the picture immediately. If you do not, I will contact my lawyer and take legal action.

*(6)*____________________________________ ,

Donald Driver

Editing : Fix the following sentences.

1. My brother works at a pizza restaurant but, he doesn't like pizza.

2. Before I go on my trip, I need to do the following things: get my passport and my plane ticket and book a hotel room.

3. His e-mail to me was too personal, he asked me how old I was and if I had a boyfriend.

4. I heard him. He said I love my job but, I love my family more.

5. What are you going to do he said?

Unit 12

Review

Unit 07 Finding a Job

Vocabulary

Read the description and write down the correct word.

Unit 12

1. When a person is looking for a job, they send this document of their work history to the company they want to work for.

2. A worker who gets along with his co-workers and tries not to fight or disagree with them is this kind of a worker.

3. Everyone always understands her whether she is speaking, e-mailing, or doing a presentation because she has these.

4. We don't like hiring students at our company because they don't have much of this.

5. Every university student must pick one of these to study.

Unit 12

Review

Grammar

Use the correct present perfect form in these sentences.

1. Have you ______________ much experience in the service industry?
2. Has she ever ______________ at a high class restaurant?
3. My boss has never ______________ a city bus before.
4. Have you ______________ my report yet? I put it on your desk.
5. She hasn't ______________ on her business trip yet. She leaves tomorrow.

Dialogue

Fill in the blanks with the correct words and practice the dialogue with your partner.

Jane: What kind of *(1)*___________ do you want after graduation?

Bob: I'm looking for something in my *(2)*___________ field of study-fashion.

Jane: Have you sent your *(3)*___________ to many companies?

Bob: Yes, I've sent it to over twenty different companies and I have three job *(4)*__________________ next week so I'm a little bit nervous.

Jane: Don't worry. You have very good communications *(5)*__________. Just make sure you wear a nice suit and maybe go and get a *(6)*___________. You hair is a bit long these days!

Bob: Thanks for your advice

Unit 08 Resume and Interview

Vocabulary

Fill in the blanks with the correct vocabulary.

1. The people I work with are my ___________________.
2. The restaurant manager's job has many ___________________ like hiring waiters and waitresses, training them, and making sure the customers are all happy.
3. I am not a manager or a boss, I am just a basic ___________________.
4. My ___________________ after finishing school is to get a job as a computer programmer at a big software company.
5. I have many good ___________________ for working in a kitchen. For example, I studied cooking in France and have worked at three very big restaurants in the past eight years.

Grammar

Change the following sentences to the passive.

1. My dog bit me.
2. The students laughed at the teacher.
3. The secretary stole the money.
4. The drunk taxi driver drove the car into the river.
5. The teacher gave the lazy student an F.

Review

Dialogue

Fill in the blanks with the correct words and practice the dialogue with your partner.

Interviewer: So Miss Kim, do you have any *(1)*____________________ working at a kindergarten?

Miss Kim: I actually haven't worked at a school before, but at my college, we had to do a work placement at a kindergarten for six months. It was a lot of fun and I really enjoyed it.

Interviewer: What are you career *(2)*____________________? Do you want to be a kindergarten teacher forever?

Miss Kim: No! But I'd like to work for at least five years and then maybe go back to school and study some more.

Interviewer: Do you have any *(3)*____________________ for us?

Miss Kim: Yes, what will my duties and *(4)*________________ be?

Interviewer: You'll have your own class of fifteen children and you'll have to organize activities for them every day, give them report cards, and meet with their parents regularly.

Unit 09 Taking Instructions On The Job

Vocabulary

Write the correct word for the following descriptions.

1. This means the same as "in a hurry" or "quickly."

2. These are the same as job benefits. For example, if you work for Korean Air, you get four free tickets every year.

3. To make everyone agree on something is this.

4. A business that never closes its doors. Like a convenience store.

5. It means the same as "arrange" a meeting.

Grammar

Take two sentences and make them into one using relative clauses.

1. Steve is a teacher. He is always helping his students.
2. I usually take the number eight subway line. It is much faster than a bus.
3. My grandmother is always cooking. She is ninety years old.
4. Shingu is a good university. It is located in Sungnam city.
5. My brother is always talking to girls. They are usually laughing at his jokes.

Dialogue

Fill in the blanks with the correct words and practice the dialogue with your partner.

Boss: Miss Lee, I need you to *(1)*____________ me a room at the Jeju Westin for Aug 21 and 22.

Miss Lee: Is it for that meeting with Hyundae? Do you want me to call them and *(2)*____________ a meeting the morning you arrive?

Boss: No, make it for the afternoon. I'm also meeting with Samsung in the morning and they seem very angry and upset with Hyundae. At the meeting, we must have *(3)*____________ or we won't be successful.

Miss Lee: Good luck with that!

Unit 10 Problems at Work

Vocabulary

Read the description and write the correct word.

1. When you get a pay raise and your job gets more responsibilities, it's because you just got a ______________.
2. Even dream jobs have good ______________ and bad ______________.
3. My co-worker always ______________ me with Spam e-mails and

stupid jokes.

4. I am ________________ and ________________ of my job. I want to quit!

5. My boss is very ________________. He is always shouting and telling people to shut up.

Grammar

Finish the following conditional sentences.

1. If I am not tired tonight……

2. If my boyfriend forgets my birthday……

3. If she hadn't driven the car while she was drunk……

4. If I had more money……

5. If I was an animal……

Unit 12

Dialogue

Fill in the blanks with the correct words and practice the dialogue with your partner.

Joe: Hey, do you like working at Google?

Sunghee: Like it, I love it. It's the perfect job. It has only *(1)*______________ and no bad points.

Joe: Really? What *(2)*______________ you come to work late?

Won't your boss be angry?

Sunghee: I never come to work *(3)*_____________ because I *(4)*_____________ my job so much!

Joe: What's so good about it?

Sunghee: If you had a job which was fun and challenging, and all of your co-workers were cool, and you didn't have to wear a suit, how *(5)*_____________ you like it?

Joe: I guess I'd like it a *(6)*_____________.

Sunghee: That's how I feel. I feel like I'm the *(7)*_____________ man alive!

Unit 11 E-mail Writing

Vocabulary

Write down the Internet slang for the following expressions.

1. For your information -
2. Please! -
3. See you! -
4. In my opinion
5. Easy-
6. Attention! -
7. Frequently Asked Questions -
8. Before

Grammar

Put the correct punctuation marks in the following sentences.

1. I went to the store and bought some apples carrots coffee and juice.
2. What do you mean? said the teacher.
3. I need the following items a notebook computer but not an Apple an MP3 player preferably with at least 4 gigs and a Samsung smart phone the Galaxy S2.
4. He needs a job with a high salary two weeks vacation a year and medical benefits.
5. She likes eating out drinking soju and going to singing rooms but not dancing at nightclubs.

Dialogue

Unit 12

Fill in the blanks with the correct dialogue.

Joe: I can't believe this e-mail.

Sue: Why? What's *(1)*_______________ with it?

Joe: It's a business e-mail and I don't really know the guy that well, but he asks be all kinds of *(2)*_______________ questions about my family and life.

Sue: Wow. That's really *(3)*_______________.

Joe: Yeah. It also has lots of *(4)*_______________ mistakes. The guy doesn't know how to use spell-check I guess.

Sue: That's really not very *(5)*_______________.

Joe: Yeah. My *(6)*_______________ of him and his company is not very good.

NEW EVERYDAY ENGLISH

Answer Key

Answer Key

Unit 01 Using a Dictionary

Warm-up

The answers depend on the dictionaries you use. The purpose it to get the students looking and comparing their answers.

Vocabulary

1. British English
2. Phrasal verb
3. Irish English
4. Idiom
5. American English
6. Something
7. Plural
8. Scottish English
9. Somebody
10. New Zealand English
11. Singular
12. Australian English

Dialogue 1

1. bookshelf
2. alphabetically
3. hurry
4. useful
5. realized

Questions

1. No.
2. When he's in a hurry.
3. Because it has more meanings, examples of usage, and sections of phrasal verbs.

Dialogue 2

Questions

1. It means to cheat on a test.
2. It means to get something you want by lying or tricking someone.
3. Examples in the dictionary.

Grammar

1. take it off
2. look at it
3. throw it away
4. turn it down
5. looking forward to it
6. make it up
7. tried it on
8. Pick it up
9. give it back
10. figure it out

Reading

Pre-reading questions are meant to stimulate interest in the reading.

Questions

1. They were missing many words, contained misspellings, and were incomplete.
2. Hundreds of scholars.
3. 20 years.
4. India, Australia, New Zealand, South Africa, and the Caribbean.

Speaking

Bread-noun
Sexy-adjective
On-preposition
Fast-adjective or adverb
Shrunk-verb
Slowly-adverb
Sometimes-adverb
Funny-adjective

1. Meaning 1: He read a good book — Meaning 2: I booked a plane ticket
2. Meaning 1: The teacher is kind — Meaning 2: Bananas are a kind of fruit
3. Meaning 1: I have a can of beer — Meaning 2: He can swim
4. Meaning 1: I watched a Broadway play — Meaning 2: Let's play cards.
5. Meaning 1: The boy is really mean. — Meaning 2: What do you mean?
6. Meaning 1: Ring the doorbell — Meaning 2: He bought her a diamond ring
7. Meaning 1: He is a dirty bum! — Meaning 2: She slapped his bum
8. Meaning 1: What a gay day! — Meaning 2: Gay marriage is legal in some countries

Editing

1. Why are you watching TV when you have homework to do? Please turn it off.
2. I'm hungry. Let's go out to eat.
3. Why are you wearing your jacket inside? Please take it off.
4. The fighting couple should make up with each other.
5. My friend lives 1 floor above me. Let's go up to his place and see what he's doing.

Unit 02 Slang and Idioms

Warm-up

1. Adage 2. Slang 3. Adage 4. Idiom 5. Slang
6. Slang 7. Idiom 8. Idiom 9. Idiom 10. Adage

Vocabulary

1. phrasal verb 2. simile 3. impress
4. realistic 5. regional 6. out-of-date
7. clear and concise 8. fluent 9. misuse
10. expressions

Dialogue 1

Questions

1. Because Wangju is using out-of-date idioms.
2. They go out-of-date quickly and they are easy to misuse.

Dialogue 2

Questions

1. To speak like a native speaker.

2. No.
3. No, but there are more useful things to learn.
4. Phrasal verbs.

Grammar

1. d 2. g 3. f 4. a 5. b 6. h 7. e 8. c

1. look forward to 2. look into 3. make (her husband) into
4. look up 5. make for 6. make up
7. look for 8. look out

Listening

1. It means you can't sleep 2. Idioms
3. Her Korean teacher 4. No
5. Simple English

Speaking

1. bat 2. horse 3. bee 4. giraffe 5. owl
6. ox 7. fox 8. peacock 9. snail 10. koala

Editing

1. You can look up his address on the internet.
2. She looked for her bag under her bed.
3. The bus driver is as slow as a snail.
4. Many classic movies aren't in color, they are in black and white.
5. My father is as busy as a bee.

Unit 03 Dialects

Warm-up

1. h) 2. a) 3. g) 4. i) 5. j)
6. c) 7. e) 8. d) 9. f) 10. b)

Answer Key

1. Goodbye
2. Bathroom or Restroom
3. Stole
4. Buy
5. Tired

Vocabulary

1. accent
2. varieties
3. expression
4. standard
5. common
6. regional
7. pronounce
8. queen's English

Dialogue 1

(1) What are you studying

(2) Is Australian English different from American English

(3) For example

(4) But why are you studying Australian English

Questions

1. A book about Australian English.
2. No, they have completely different dialects the pronunciation and expressions are both different.
3. Yes, because he's going to visit Australia and he's going to work in a resort where many Australian tourists go.

Dialogue 2

(1) dialects (2) well (3) accents (4) not (5) then

(6) speaking (7) native (8) heavy (9) important (10) standard

Questions

1. Because there are so many dialects to learn.
2. To work in the hotel industry.
3. If you are going to live in the country or work in a place where the dialect is used.

Grammar

1. There - place
2. Yesterday - time
3. Sometimes - frequency
4. Upstairs - place
5. Quickly - manner
6. Often - frequency AND Slowly manner
7. Late - time
8. Fast - manner
9. Quite - degree
10. Now - time

Suggested answers

1. I live near the school
2. She came late to class
3. He is pretty smart
4. The teacher arrived early
5. Go straight and turn left

Reading

(Answers may vary.)

Speaking

Student A. cheeky-samrtass windscreen-car wind shield git-idiot knickers-panties/under wear lorry-truck

Student B. fairdinkum-fair or true yobbo-thug heaps-lots pommy-Englishman sunnies-suglasse

Editing

1. She woke up late today.
2. My grandmother is very kind.
3. He ran fast all the way to school.
4. I hardly ever smoke cigarettes.
5. The students changed clothes very fast.

Unit 04 Pronunciation

Warm-up

The answers are very subjective and should be discussed as a class

Answer Key

Vocabulary

1. 음성학 **2.** 강세 **3.** 모음 **4.** 자음
5. 억양 **6.** 발음 **7.** 음절 **8.** 유창한

1. fluent **2.** vowels, consonants **3.** syllables
4. pronunciation **5.** phonetics **6.** stress
7. intonation

Dialogue 1

Questions

1. To help improve her listening and speaking.
2. To speak perfectly like a native speaker.
3. Henry Kissinger and Gimoon Ban.

1. language **2.** dictionary **3.** overseas **4.** university
5. soccer **6.** theater **7.** t-shirt **8.** octopus

Dialogue 2

Questions

1. Because the meaning of a word changes if the stress is different.
2. In a dictionary.

1. PhotOgraphy **2.** PhOtograph **3.** DiAlects
4. Evil **5.** KorEAn **6.** RecOrding
7. BlAckboard **8.** DIAmond

Grammar

1. The book was really interesting.
2. Mr. Gibson, can you help me? Actually, my name is Mr. Olson.
3. I only gave my phone number to one boy OR I gave my phone.

number to only one boy.

4. I didn't like the concert either.
5. Byungchan really likes Haesu. Really? Youngju really likes her too.
6. When we walked outside, suddenly, it began to rain.
7. When my grandfather felt pain in his chest I immediately called an ambulance.
8. My best friend and I went to school.
9. I lost my wallet last night. Fortunately, somebody found it and gave it to the police.
10. My friends all love singing, especially Minsu.

Listening

1a. You like Rains music and Rain's movies.

1b. You like Rains music and all movies.

2a. He is good looking but that is not why you are dating him.

2b. You aren't dating him because he is not good-looking.

3a. You are asking your mom to eat together.

3b. You are asking your brother or sister to eat your mother together.

4a. If you don't have a boyfriend or husband, your life has no meaning.

4b. If a boy doesn't have a wife or girlfriend, his life has no meaning.

5a. One girl name MaryJane went to school with you.

5b. Two girls, Mary and Jane, went to school with you.

Speaking

1. No, I went to the library yesterday night.
2. No, I have one brother.
3. No, it's his sister.
4. No, I bought the red sweater.
5. No, I said my father is a doctor.
6. No and want you to call John or Peter, not both.
7. No, I'm learning Chinese.
8. No, I'm going to America to travel.
9. No, he's always reading novels.
10. No, it's Suzie.

Conversation 1

A. ↑
B. ↓ ↓
A. ↑
B. ↑
A. ↓
B. ↓
A. ↓

Conversation 2

A. ↓
B. ↓
A. ↑ ↑
B. ↓
A. ↑
B. ↓

Editing

1. I really enjoyed the TV show.
2. I will never smoke cigarettes.
3. I usually go to the nightclub OR I sometimes go to the nightclub.
4. He only drinks on Saturday night.
5. She sometimes leaves her home before 7a.m.

Unit 05 Konglish

Warm-up

1. drunken - GM
2. booking - K
3. more better looking - GM
4. sign - K
5. A
6. buy an apartment - K
7. panties - K
8. played the computer - GM
9. stressful - GM
10. A

Vocabulary

1. coined
2. Aawkward
3. borrowed words
4. contraction
5. meaning
6. misuse
7. abbreviation
8. collocation

Dialogue 1

(1) native (2) ex-pats (3) consistently (4) be careful

Questions

1. Surprised.
2. He likes it.
3. When she travels or lives abroad.

Dialogue 2

(1) studying (2) coins (3) funny (4) changed

Questions

1. Because he finds it interesting and fun.
2. It coins new words, and abbreviates words.
3. She thought Konglish was bad English.
4. She thinks Konglish is good.

Grammar

1. Heirloom 2. Nuclear 3. Only 4. Distant
5. Elder 6. Raise 7. Reunion 8. Single
9. Punish 10. Do

Travel Collocations

1. abroad or Overseas 2. guide
3. package 4. scuba
5. missed

Listening

(1) embarrassed (2) proud
(3) languages (4) coin
(5) different (6) future
(7) borrowed (8) changed
(9) understand (10) dialect
(11) ashamed

Answer Key

Questions

1. Embarrassed
2. No. They don't
3. No, it isn't. It is used consistently
4. Another dialect
5. ____________

Speaking

1. Hotchkiss - stapler
2. Meeting - blind date
3. Gagman - comedian AND backdancer - dancer
4. Backmirror - rearview mirror AND handle - steering wheel AND punc flat tire
5. One-piece - dress AND panties - underwear
6. Live - draft AND cider - 7-up or Sprite
7. Cunning - cheating
8. McGuyve - Swiss Army
9. Lover - girlfriend AND hunt - pick up
10. Service - on the house OR free AND glamour - glamorous

Editing

1. I like to take a shower before I go to bed.
2. The pilot flies the airplane two weeks every month.
3. The casino dealer has to mix the cards before he deals them to the players.
4. My mother cooks very delicious kimbap.
5. My car won't start because the battery is dead.

Unit 06 Review units 01-05

Unit 01 Using a Dictionary

Vocabulary

1. Something
2. New Zealand English
3. Singular
4. American English
5. Phrasal verb
6. Somebody
7. Plural
8. British English

Grammar

1. give it back
2. looking forward to
3. turn on
4. pick up
5. try on

Dialogue

(1) use
(2) electronic
(3) why
(4) examples
(5) learn
(6) verbs

Unit 02 Slang and Idioms

Vocabulary

1. fluent
2. phrasal verb
3. regional
4. out-of-date
5. clear and concise

Grammar

1. Looking forward to
2. Look out
3. Look it up
4. Making for
5. Looking into

Dialogue

(1) wasting
(2) spend
(3) useful
(4) important
(5) impresses
(6) misuses
(7) native
(8) realistic

Unit 03 Dialects

Vocabulary

1. pronounce
2. accent
3. regional
4. standard
5. common

Answer Key

Grammar

1. there - place
2. last night - time
3. sometimes - frequency
4. upstairs - location
5. quickly - manner
6. slowly - manner
7. late - manner
8. fast - manner
9. quite - degree
10. now - time

Dialogue

(1) about **(2)** different **(3)** friend **(4)** reasons

Unit 04 Pronunciation

Vocabulary

1. Consonants
2. Fluent
3. Phonics
4. Syllable
5. Pronunciation
6. Intonation
7. Vowels
8. Stress

Grammar

1. He is a really interesting person.
2. Are you a teacher? Actually, I'm a student.
3. I only studied one hour for the test.
4. I didn't like the pizza. Really? I didn't like it either.
5. You like ice cream? Me too!

Dialogue

(1) What are you studying
(2) phonetic
(3) fluently
(4) native

Unit 05 Konglish

Vocabulary

1. borrowed
2. contractions
3. definition
4. collocations
5. borrowed

Grammar

1. Hard
2. Beautiful
3. Funny
4. Fresh
5. Oral

Dialogue

(1) eye
(2) Konglish
(3) uses
(4) English
(5) dialects
(6) taught
(7) awkward

Unit 07 Finding a Job

Warm-up

(Answers may vary.)

Vocabulary

(1) ideal candidate
(2) team player
(3) communication skills
(4) effective
(5) Basic to intermediate
(6) Experience
(7) major
(8) ambitious
(9) growth potential
(10) resume

Grammer

1. I have applied for many jobs recently.
   Usage Meaning: used when the time is recent.
2. James has gone for many job interviews since 2007.
   Usage Meaning: used to talk about actions that continue from the past to the present.
3. What have you learned from your other jobs?

Usage Meaning: used to talk about actions that continue from the past to the present.

4. No thank you. I have just had a cup of coffee.
   Usage Meaning: used when the time is recent.
5. Kim has worked here for 10 years.
   Usage Meaning: talk about actions that continue from the past to the present.

Reading

1. C
2. The five-star hotel prefers people with management experience.
3. A university degree is necessary.
4. The eligible candidate can start to work as a day-trip tour guide immediately.
5. You need to visit the company's website if you want to apply for this job.
6. (Answers may vary.)

Editing

1. She has not read the email yet.
2. I have never been on a business trip.
3. Has Karl had a job interview at CJ Corporation yet?
4. We've still not eaten our dinner.
5. They've already chosen someone for the position.

Unit 08 Resume and Interview

Warm-up

(Answers may vary.)

Similar	Different
Include basic personal information : name, address, contact number, and email address	In an English resume, social security number, gender, birth date, picture, height, weight, blood type, religion, army duties, family information are not included
Special licenses, certificates, work experiences are included.	

Vocabulary

1. l **2.** a **3.** j **4.** b
5. g **6.** h **7.** k **8.** f
9. c **10.** d **11.** i **12.** e

Dialogue

1. Ms. Moon chose Shingu Hospital because it is a place where she can apply her skills and further develop her experience and knowledge.

2. Ms. Moon used what she learned at school and helped the elderly and disabled children with their mobility at her volunteer place.

3. (Answers may vary.)

Grammar

A. **1.** Matt was excited by the news.

2. Did his parents get excited by the news?

3. The employment contract was signed by Sunny.

4. Were you asked to sign the contract, too, by the CEO?

5. The acceptance letter to newly hired employees was faxed by the secretary.

B. My first job as a radiologist

(1) was hired **(2)** was shared
(3) was burdened **(4)** were assisted
(5) were given **(6)** was performed
(7) were reported **(8)** was given

Answer Key

Listening

- **(1)** describe yourself
- **(2)** If I get this job
- **(3)** goals
- **(4)** established
- **(5)** a goal-oriented
- **(6)** achieve my goals
- **(7)** set a goal
- **(8)** college experience
- **(9)** a business career
- **(10)** concentrate
- **(11)** part-time job
- **(12)** influenced
- **(13)** this career
- **(14)** past experiences
- **(15)** hire
- **(16)** passionate
- **(17)** put forth great effort
- **(18)** successful

Speaking and Writing

(Answers may vary.)

Editing

1. The students were taught to write a good resume.
2. John was interviewed by the manager.
3. Where is the job advertisement posted in the bulletin boards?
4. The dinner was served to newly hired employees.
5. The welcoming speech was given by the CEO of the company.

Unit 09 Taking Instructions On The Job

Vocabulary Exercises

1. 24-7
2. minutes
3. in a jiffy
4. perks
5. set up
6. book
7. consensus
8. point out
9. as well
10. zero tolerance policy

Dialogue

(1) referring **(2)** takeover **(3)** set up
(4) consensus **(5)** interrupt **(6)** perks
(7) book **(8)** regarding

Grammar Exercises

1. whom **2.** whose **3.** who
4. that **5.** which **6.** who
7. whose **8.** who **9.** that
10. who

Compreheasion

1. 24-7
2. Asks her to stay late, calls her "dear", sits close to her
3. sexual harassment
4. Zero tolerance
5. colleges, company officies, hospitals, laboratories, and in the service industry

Editing

1. I want to talk to the person that is in charge.
2. I saw the doctor whom you told me about.
3. Did you find the dog that you lost.
4. I ran a marathon, which was my third full-length marathon, last week.
5. Is he the boy whose parents won the lottery?

Unit 10 Problems at Work

Vocabulary

1. e **2.** i **3.** a
4. d **5.** b **6.** h
7. f **8.** j **9.** c
10. g

Answer Key

1. sick and tired 2. current 3. perks
4. pros and cons 5. promotion 6. rude

Dialogue 1

1. He works long hours.
2. Talk to his boss.
3. No, he's just traditional and he works longer hours than John.
4. No, he's worked there for more than 5 years.
5. No.

Dialogue 2

1. The passengers are rude.
2. No.
3. They never listen, they never say please or thank you, they get drunk and harass other passengers.
4. They sexually harass flight attendants.
5. She is too short.

Grammar

Practice 1

1. will 2. will 3. have been
4. won't 5. would 6. will
7. have become 8. will quit 9. will
10. will

Practice 2

1. f 2. h 3. g
4. a 5. j 6. c
7. i 8. d 9. e
10. b

Listing

Megumi Yamaguchi

1. She is a hairdresser and works in Shinjuku
2. She meets interesting people and enjoys her job but is tired from working on her feet all day and the shop is very small

Dareen McDonald

1. A bartender at the Hyatt
2. They like to talk
3. The working hours
4. At his bar

Sarah Anderson

1. A computer programmer
2. She likes solving problems and working with computer but there aren't enough women working as programmers
3. Because of her boss

Unit 11 E-mail Writing

Warm-up

1. Before
2. For your information
3. Frequently asked questions
4. Easy
5. In my opinion
6. Oh my God
7. Please
8. Age, sex, location
9. Attention
10. See you

Vocabulary

1. emoticons
2. typo

3. personal
4. impression
5. contact information
6. slang
7. Professional
8. punctuation
9. weird
10. informal

Dialogue 1

(1) strange
(2) jackets
(3) weekend
(4) spelling
(5) questions
(6) professional

Questions

1. Strange.
2. It was too personal and had many spelling and punctuation mistakes, and emoticons.
3. He wasn't professional.

Dialogue 2

(1) consise
(2) wordy
(3) punctuation
(4) impression
(5) title
(6) personal
(7) depends

Questions

1. Yes.
2. Your name, job title, and contact information.
3. No. It depends on how well you know the person you are writing.
4. Your e-mail address.

Grammar

1. f
2. g
3. a
4. d
5. c
6. b
7. h
8. e

Practice

Put commas in the correct place

1. I don't like working overtime, but sometimes you have to do it.
2. In her free time, my mother enjoys cooking, reading, and watching movies.
3. For my next test I won't be able to study as much, but I will pass it.
4. My boyfriend his sister, and I went to Namdaemun market last night.
5. I didn't eat anything, but I have a stomachache.

Put colons and semi-colons in the correct place

1. My father enjoys any of the following things: jogging, hiking, drinking with his friends, and playing go-stop.
2. He gets upset when people ask him about his age; he is very sensitive.
3. On my last trip to Europe, I visited the following places: London, England; Paris, France; and Rome, Italy.
4. Korean high school students study 24 hours a day; they never get any sleep.
5. My mother is the glue that keeps our family together; without her we'd break apart.

Put double or single quotation marks in the correct place

1. My girlfriend asked me, "Are you going to marry me?"
2. I heard my boss talking. He said, "If it's not broke, don't fix it."
3. "Look", he said "she told him, 'I don't love you,' and she also said, 'I never want to see you again."
4. "Oh no!" he cried, "I left my bag on the subway."
5. Einstein said, "God does not play with dice."

Reading

Dear John,

I'm really sorry I didn't write you back sooner but I've been very busy at work. Here are the answers to the questions in your e-mail:

What winter clothes do we sell? We specialize in ski clothes including jackets, pants, gloves, scarves and hats.

How long would it take for a large shipment to be delivered? We guarantee delivery in less than 4 working days.

Do we give bulk discounts? For orders of more than 5000 units, we give 7% off and for orders of 10,000 or more, we give 12% off.

If you have any more questions, please let us know.

Sincerely,

Paul Smith

Speaking

1. e **2.** c **3.** d
4. f **5.** b **6.** a

(1) To whom it may concern
(2) in regards to
(3) It has come to my attention
(4) I was disappointed
(5) I would appreciate it if
(6) Sincerely

Editing

1. My brother works at a pizza restaurant, but he doesn't like pizza
2. Before I go on my trip, I need to do the following things: get my passport and plane ticket, and book a hotel room
3. His e-mail to me was too personal; he asked how old I was and if I had

a boyfriend.

4. I heard him. He said, 'I love my job but I love my family more.'
5. "What are you going to do?" he said.

Unit 12 Review Units 07-11

Unit 07 Finding a Job

Vocabulary

1. Resume
2. Teamplayer
3. Communication skills
4. Experience
5. A major

Grammar

1. had
2. worked
3. ridden
4. seen
5. gone

Dialogue

(1) job
(2) major
(3) resume
(4) interviews
(5) skills
(6) haircut

Unit 08 Resume and Interview

Vocabulary

1. Co-workers
2. responsibilities
3. Employee
4. objective
5. qualifications

Answer Key

Grammar

1. I was bitten by my dog.
2. The teacher was laughed at by the students.
3. The money was stolen by the secretary.
4. The car was driven into the river by the drunk taxi driver.
5. The lazy student was given an F by the teacher.

Dialogue

(1) experience **(2)** objectives
(3) questions **(4)** responsibilities

Unit 09 Taking Instructions On the Job

Vocabulary

1. In a jiffy
2. Perks
3. Consensus
4. 24-7
5. Set up

Grammar

1. Steve is a teacher who is always helping his students
2. I usually take the number 1 line which is much faster than a bus
3. My grandmother who is 90 years old is always cooking
4. Shingu is a good university which is located in Sungnam city
5. My brother is always talking to girls who are usually laughing at his jokes

Dialogue

(1) book **(2)** set up **(3)** consensus

Unit 10 Problems at Work

Vocabulary

1. promotion
2. points, points
3. annoys
4. sick, tired
5. rude/impolite

Grammar

1. I'll meet my friends.
2. I'll be very angry.
3. She wouldn't have gotten in the accident.
4. I'd buy a car.
5. I'd be a tiger.

Dialogue

(1) good points
(2) if
(3) late
(4) love
(5) would
(6) lot
(7) luckiest

Unit 11 E-mail Writing

Vocabulary

1. FYI
2. PlZ
3. CYA
4. OMO
5. EZ
6. Attn
7. FAQ
8. B4

Grammar

1. I went to the store and bought some apples, carrots, coffee, and juice.
2. "What do you mean?" said the teacher.
3. need the following items: a notebook computer, but not an Apple; an MP3 player, preferably with at least 4 gigs; and a Samsung smart phone, the Galaxy 2.
4. He needs a job with a high salary, two weeks vacation a year, and medical benefits.
5. She likes eating out, drinking soju, and going to singing rooms, but not dancing at nightclubs.

Answer Key

Dialogue

(1) wrong

(2) personal

(3) strange/weird

(4) spelling

(5) professional

(6) impression

NEW EVERYDAY ENGLISH

Listening Scripts

Unit 02 Slang and Idioms

Jieun: Morning Chris.

Chris: Morning Jieun. Hey, what's wrong? You look so tired.

Jieun: I am. Last night I was turning and tossing all night long.

Chris: You were turning and tossing? I think you mean tossing and turning.

Jieun: Oh no! I'm always making mistakes when I use English.

Chris: Misusing idioms is very easy. Sometimes it's better to just speak simply. Instead of "tossing and turning", just say, "I didn't sleep well last night." It means the same thing.

Jieun: But it sounds more natural to say "tossing and turning."

Chris: Well, maybe a bit, but using simple English is better because it's harder to misuse it. Plus all speakers of English native speakers and non-native speakers will be able to understand you.

Jieun: But my Korean teacher said idioms are important.

Chris: If you're going to live in a foreign country, you'll get plenty of opportunities to hear the regional idioms and expressions. But if you plan on staying in Korea, you'll be using English with a variety of different English speakers. Learning all of the idioms for every country isn't realistic.

Jieun: I guess you're right. Thanks for the advice.

Unit 05 Konglish

Many Koreans feel embarrassed when they hear foreigners talk about Konglish. Others feel proud and enjoy using Konglish. Is Konglish bad English? Many linguists don't think so. All languages are always changing and evolving. People stop using some vocabulary and coin new words and expressions. The English used 100 years ago is very different than the English we use today. And the English in the future is going to be different too.

The English language has borrowed thousands of words from other languages. The definition of many words has changed too. Korean English is doing the same thing. As long as the words and expressions are used consistently and people understand what the words mean, it is not bad English, it is becoming another dialect of English, like Singapore or Philippine English. Koreans should never feel ashamed of using Konglish.

Unit 08 Resume and Interview

1. How would you describeyourself?

I majored in Tax Accounting from Shingu University. I don't like my major but my parents wanted me to become an accountant. I am obedient, so now I'm applying for this position. If I get this job, my parents will be very happy.

2. What specific goals have you established for your life?

I am a goal-oriented person. I work really hard to achieve my goals. So, I have always achieved the goals I have set. More importantly, I set my goals carefully and realistically. For example, I set a goal to graduate with good grades, and I graduated top of my class.

3. How has your college experience prepared you for a business career?

Sorry, I am not prepared because I've never had a job. I just wanted to concentrate on my studies, so I didn't even have a part-time job.

4. What influenced you to choose this career?

My past experiences have shown me that I enjoy serving others. I really love helping others. When people I helped are happy, it makes me feel important. That's why I have chosen this career.

5. Why should we hire you?

I should be hired because I am passionate and ready to do whatever you want me to do. I will put forth great effort to be one of the most successful and proud employees of this company.

Unit 10 Problems at Work

Job 1

My name is Megumi Yamaguchi and I work at a hair salon in Shinjuku. I am a hairdresser. I love my job because I get to meet a lot of really interesting people and I really enjoy working on people's hair and making them look better. Of course no job is perfect and there are some things I really hate about my job. First, I'm on my feet all day and get really tired.

At the end of my day, my feet are really sore! I also get tired of working in such a small area. If I could work in a bigger shop, I'd be a lot happier. Mostly, my customers love me, but once in a while, I get a bad customer who complains about the hair cut. I hate it when the customers are rude and I have to smile and be polite.

Job 2

My name is Darren McDonald and I'm a bartender at the Hyatt Cheapskate Pub. Being a bartender is fun. If people ask me what I like about the job, I tell them I enjoy meeting and talking to the customers. Most people who come to my pub are very nice and friendly and like to talk. I like meeting new people and listening to their stories, so it's a perfect job for me. The only thing I don't like about my job are the working hours. I usually work until 3am. By the time I get home it's after 4 and I'm usually in bed by 5am. I eat my breakfast at 1pm and then start work at 7pm, so it's tough to find time to meet my old friends. They have to come to my bar if they want to see me!

Job 3

I'm Sarah Anderson and I work as a computer programmer. I love the challenge of problem solving and working with computers so my job is really perfect for my character. If there is one negative thing, I wish more women worked as computer programmers. Most of my coworkers are men and all of my bosses have been men and a lot of them aren't comfortable about working with a woman as a computer programmer. My current boss has been really hard to work for and I feel a bit uncomfortable working with him because he's always making rude jokes, so I'm looking for a job at another company.

English Textbook Committee

Bae, Yoondo (Shingu College)
Robert Gibson (Shingu College)
Sunna Yang (Shingu College)

NEW EVERYDAY ENGLISH Book 4

PUBLISHED BY SHINGU PUBLISHING CO.
2661 geumkwang-dong, jungwon-gu, seongnam-si, gyeonggi-do, Korea
Tel. 031-741-3055, 3056 Fax. 031-741-3054

First Published 2012
Printed in seoul, Korea.

ISBN 978-89-7668 190-4 03740